KEYWORDS | Gender

THE KEYWORDS SERIES

Identity

Truth

Gender

Experience

KEYWORDS | Gender

OTHER

Other Press • New York

Copyright © 2004 Alliance of Independent Publishers, France

First published in China by Shanghai Literature and Art Publishing House
First published in France by Éditions La Découverte
First published in India by Sage India
First published in Morocco and Lebanon by Arab Cultural Center of
Casablanca/Beirut
First published in South Africa by Double Storey Books
First published in the United States by Other Press, New York

Production Editor: Robert D. Hack
Text design: Kaoru Tamura and Natalya Balnova

This book was set in Joanna MT by Alpha Graphics of Pittsfield, NH.

10 9 8 7 6 5 4 3 2 1

Library of Congress Cataloging-in-Publication Data

Keywords: gender / Linda Waldman . . . [et al.].
      p. cm.
   Includes bibliographical references.
   ISBN 1-59051-107-7 (pbk. : alk. paper)
   1. Sex role–Cross-cultural studies.   2. Gender
identity–Cross-cultural studies.   3. Sexism–Cross-cultural studies.   4.
Feminist theory. I. Waldman, Linda.
HQ1075.K49 2004
305.3–dc22

                                                              2004006504

CONTENTS

SERIES PREFACE

Established on the initiative of the Charles Leopold Mayer Foundation, the KEYWORDS collection was born of a propitious encounter between a Chinese, an American, and a French publisher. The project is now being executed by the Alliance of Independent Publishers[1] that, besides its founders—Shanghai Cultural Publishers and La Découverte in France—includes Double Storey Books in South Africa, Le Centre Cultural Arabe in Casablanca and Beirut, Other Press in the United States, and Sage Publications India. The project offers fundamental notions from different cultural points of view, taking a hard look at a common object with a view from afar. The collection thereby aims to produce an intercultural dialogue and an exploration of globalization with, as point of departure, local points of

---

1. See www.fph.ch and www.alliance-editeurs.org

view on essential themes such as *experience, gender* (or masculine-feminine), *identity, nature,* and *truth*. Thus, in their respective languages, the publishers will provide the same small book on one of the words chosen beforehand, and each will then consist of six articles of about twenty pages each. For example, the notion of *truth* will, in turn, be tackled by an African, an American, an Arab, a Chinese, and an Indian writer, each of whose texts will then be translated into four languages respectively: English, Arabic, Chinese, and French. The texts will be exchanged between the publishers to come out under the same title within the same year in each of the countries in question. In short: one word and six points of view to create, if not a world, at least a book.

Such a new and difficult project had to proclaim its experimental character with all that this implies as source but also as experimentation and approximation. Furthermore, it needed a pragmatic framework and a few guiding, though equally flexible, principles. Then there was the choice of words. For some of these, we were concerned with current events, taking into account major political considerations, examinations divided along the line of contemporary debate in the terms and contexts of expression that are frequently misunderstood. The questions of *identity* and *gender* became imperative: these past few decades they have heavily mobilized public opinion and the academy. They are keywords that now circulate almost everywhere and deserve to be torn from the untrammeled use they so often get. They have gained from being set free from the ambiguities and globalizations that render them meaningless.

Obviously, the glitter of the topical is better understood when supported by a few historical and semantic reference points. By backing this up with symbolic patterns and antecedents, one can better define the outlines and what is at stake, check off implicit comparisons and their imaginary hierarchical

organizations, and get rid of old references that add up like hast-
ily assembled arrangements. Thus, the false familiarities and
simultaneities, spun by the media networks, are seen more
clearly. In this plural space that has no center, in which the
suggestions may intersect or be ignored or excluded, the confrontation can only hold surprises. The map of problems, their
formulation, the development of ideas, the range of preoccu-
pations, the levels of historicity and abstraction, and the degree
of intensity necessarily fluctuate. Hybridizations are not always
recognized and identity fixations are not always where one
expects to find them. Gaps of temporality run through the
various societies themselves (and not just across borders) by
crystallizing other forms of discontinuity. The unspoken is at
least as significant as what is presented.

The complexity of the transmissions can never be sufficiently
assessed; therefore, the translations pose an immediate problem.
The concept of *gender*, which has nurtured entire departments
in the English-speaking universities and has henceforth been
adopted by international organizations, has always been the
object of controversy. It is of concern today in the United States
where it was born and spread, although not without polemics
in the feminist camp itself, because of the problematics of
transgender and queer. The Arab author will clasp it to do a
libertarian rereading of the past and brilliantly serve the cause
of women and homosexuals. As for the famous question of *identity*, which in its various modalities does not stop troubling poli-
ticians today, it has exciting extensions depending on whether
it is reopened to a very refined question on colonialism (Africa)
or refers to a game of mirrors and paradoxical deconstruction
that ends up as a transcultural demand (China); whether it lends
itself to a wholesome de-dramatization (on the side of the
Arabs) and a swinging back of the pendulum in the United
States as a reaction to earlier multiculturalism; or whether it is

simply the opportunity provided here to clearly expose the terms and turns of the debate (in India and Europe).

Other concepts, if not more classical and timeless, ask to be presented when they structure worlds, that is to say when they are articulated orders but also, for many people today, a haven on the horizon of a daily life in flux. Above all, when they turn out not to be any less problematic than the first ones: What is *nature* today? How did the Arab philosophers rethink the *physis* of Aristotle or the neo-Platonists and what advantage did the theologians take of this to fight them? How does *experience* issue forth from event in China and in what way is it inexpressible? Is it still pertinent to oppose scientific *experience*, the experience lived in psychoanalytic treatment, with what Kant calls the "judgment of experience"? Why has this term acquired such imaginary bulk in the portrayal that America has of itself? By what alternate routes have we moved from one model of mathematical *truth* and universal forms of what is *true* to a pluralization, indeed its disappearance as thematic in the order of the techno-sciences? How do we report in just a few pages on *truth* according to the Vedas, the Upanishads, the great epics, Shankara, the poetic theory of Bharata, the mystic songs of the *Bhakta*, and the Gandhian ideal? The history of ideas is not an insignificant exercise, especially in a limited space and for the benefit of the other who is presumed to be ignorant—or almost ignorant—of the background. Obviously, there will only be a few lines of demarcation here allowing for the decoding of a cultural landscape or of daily life, roughly outlining the genealogy of a philosophical question, and here and there letting the game of theoretic uncoupling or loans be guessed at.

It may happen that an author decides to ignore the historical side of a concept in order to focus on a reality that stands out: How and within what boundaries did the South African Truth and Reconciliation Commission operate? Generally, however, the

issues have been put in perspective by being directed at an au-
dience abroad and also by letting everyone hear the novelty of
his or her own voice in hitherto unpublished combinations. In
the absence or well nigh absence of a preliminary designation
(methodological, epistemological, political, and so forth) the
space that becomes visible is not without relief or accidents. Some
articles may well seem too "technical," others not sufficiently
so. From one region to another, they differ in their levels of
analysis and more generally in their disciplinary approaches: the
Chinese and the Arabs pay special attention to language; Indians
like to think of themselves as sociologists or anthropologists; the
plural disciplines of the American cultural studies differ from those
of the French philosophers. These texts, which are neither ency-
clopedic articles nor free essays, have the value of being docu-
ments: they do not aspire to being strictly representative (of a
state of knowledge, a discipline, an identity) and no institution
mandated them, smoothed them out, or standardized them. Speaking for themselves, they call more than anything else for being
discussed, studied, and augmented. It is left up to the readers to
pursue the thinking, to immerse themselves in the different
points of view to try to compare and flush out the dissimilarities or the common values. We are here concerned merely with
providing some insights, with preparing an encounter, and open-
ing a space to make contact.

The choice of authors was also the object of a few minimal
guidelines. Priority was given to authors—philosophers, lin-
guists, sociologists, anthropologists, and so on—from the South
of the various cultural regions concerned rather than to those
who live in the West. In this first series we did not always manage it, but for the most part this will be the case. Moreover,
we have attempted to act in such a way as to avoid two stum-
bling blocks, each of which would misrepresent the project and
both of which are well known since they feed the debate on

globalization today. On the one hand, we had to avoid specific characteristics that were too great, whether it concerned terminology that was too specialized, subjective idiosyncrasies, or closed attitudes expressing a denial of the other. Although it is true that we do not all support certain political positions that are expressed here and there, on the whole we fulfilled this condition. On the other hand, we were not to give in to the standardization resulting from certain contemporary infatuations: identity withdrawal or mimetic reencoding in conformity with forms of a too-marked postmodern rhetoric. The collection rests on processes of scholarly circulation, the growing internationalization of research that solicited and stimulated it. It has updated a third more or less compact space corresponding to themes and regions that divert or complicate the dichotomies between dominators and dominated. Without this implicit theoretical horizon, the complex game of appropriations, occasional restrictions, and gaps that one sees emerge from one article to another, would not have been possible.

The achievement of these small books owes a great deal to the loyal support from and help of Etienne Galliand, to whom herewith our gratitude. We also wish to express our sincere thanks to Jean Copans, Françoise Cremel, Ghislaine Glasson Deschaumes, Thomas Keenan, Michèle Ignazzi, Michel Izard, Farouk Mardam-Bey, Ramona Naddaff, Jean-Luc Racine, and Roshi Rashed.

Nadia Tazi
Paris, November 2003

Translated by Marjolijn de Jager

from *Africa*

GRIQUATOWN *BOORLINGS* AND *INKOMMERS*

———

Linda Waldman

Now the tension, they are your enemy in the family because you are an inkommer and they say you are getting rich here. (Interview, Eddie Fortuin and Erick Scholtz, August 20, 1997)

THIS ARTICLE EXPLORES THE themes of gender and status in Griquatown, South Africa. Located in the center of the Northern Cape, Griquatown is a small, economically depressed rural town on the historical site of the nineteenth-century London Missionary Society (LMS) mission to the Griqua people. By the late twentieth century, the occupants of Griquatown comprised a complex mix of people who, while all South African citizens, still referred back to the racial structure of former apartheid South Africa and often identified themselves as colored, black, or white. There were descendants of the original mission converts, who saw themselves as Griqua (also designated a subcategory of the colored population during apartheid) and who simultaneously argued that they were *boorlings*, "people born to Griquatown." In calling themselves *boorlings*, they distinguished between themselves and those people who had recently moved to the town. The term *boorlings* is a Griquatown variant of the technically correct Afrikaans word, *inboorlinge*, which means "those born to an area." It also means birthright and residential status. Newcomers, in contrast to *boorlings*, were known as *inkommers*, or, more literally, "those who have come in" (West 1971, p. 12) and who, by implication, had no birthright in the town.

An examination of the ways in which people used these two concepts reveals much about the gendered relationships in Griquatown. The terms *inkommers* and *boorlings* had significance on two levels. First, they defined a broad ethnic identity. Being Griqua was thought of in terms of belonging to Griquatown. *Inkommers* could not be of Griquatown and therefore could not cast themselves as Griqua. Griqua men were thus seen as *boorlings* when interacting with newcomers who were predominantly, but not exclusively, male. This relationship between men identified as either *boorlings* or newcomers is explored in the first part of this article. The second part explores the relationship between Griqua men and Griqua women and, in so doing, examines the second usage of the terms *boorling* and *inkommer*, in which the focus is narrowed to the level of intra-Griqua relations. Men born of Griquatown were often seen as *inkommers* in relation to their wives and mothers-in-law. This was because being Griqua was something that women stressed through initiation and other rituals and through asserting their control of the home. Through ritual, women reinforced their identity as genuine initiated Griquas and symbolized men's outsider status in women's homes and, by implication, to being Griqua. This double use of the terms *inkommer* and *boorling* suggests that the categories were themselves ambiguous and that they reflect a society in which relationships between men and women were more complex than immediately apparent.

Not only were these categories *boorling* and *inkommer* ambiguous, they were also flexible and open to manipulation. This situation is not unique in South Africa. In Port Nolloth, West (1971) argues that *inkommers* were determined in terms of geographic distance, kin relationships, and how extensively people visited the town in their youth. Similarly, Boonzaier (1984) demonstrated that *inkommers* to the Richtersveld downplayed their cultural differences until they acquired full citizenship rights. In Namibia, Pearson (1986) shows how historical waves of immigration into Rehoboth have affected the categorization of people as *inkommers* and *boorlings*, since earlier *inkommers* married local residents and became part of the community. As the following sections show, in Griquatown such interactions between *boorlings* and *inkommers* were also not sharply defined. A *boorling* identity, however, did act to limit *inkommers* opportunities to claim a Griqua identity.

MEN AS *BOORLINGS:* RELATIONS
WITH MALE OUTSIDERS

Although Griquatown society was profoundly affected by the apartheid doctrine (1948–1994) that segregated whites, coloreds, and blacks, the category of coloreds retained an internal classification scheme that reflected some indigenous pastoral, or Khoi, values and customs. Many men, although designated colored, considered themselves to be Griqua *boorlings*, hence emphasizing their birthright to Griquatown and its society. They contrasted their part-colored, part-Griqua identity to that of *inkommers*, who, although born elsewhere in South Africa, were resident in Griquatown for career reasons. Belonging to Griqua-town was an important source of status, given the historic foundation of the town as a mission station where, in the nineteenth century, proud, independent, and wealthy Griqua *Kapteins* (captains) ruled in conjunction with the LMS missionaries. As the following example makes clear, this was especially pertinent to descendants of the *Kapteins*: Andries Waterboer I was the first Christian *Kaptein* of Griquatown (1820–1852) and his leadership, aided by missionary support, linked Christianity to Griqua identity. His great grandson, Nicolaas Waterboer II, was the last acknowledged *Kaptein* of Griquatown and he established the Griqua People's Organization [GPO, discussed below]. After the fall of apartheid, the Captaincy was revived and Nicolaas's nephew, Andries Waterboer, acquired this title in the late 1990s (Waldman 2001). However, Andries regarded his title with ambivalence[1] and later handed leadership over to his younger brother. He felt no need to assert himself as a significant individual and leader. In part, this came from his sense of historic importance: as the nephew of Nicolaas Waterboer, he was acutely aware of his proud heritage and of how they had suffered when apartheid legislation was implemented. In part, it stemmed from his socioeconomic circumstances as a builder with several teams of men working for him and sufficient work to keep him busy for several years.[2] Because he was a Waterboer, and descended from the historic *Kapteins* around whom Griquatown was formed, Andries was the quintessential *boorling* in the positive sense of the word.

Andries Waterboer was unusual in Griquatown in that he was a *boorling* who had done relatively well. Within apartheid South Africa—a highly industrialized and capitalist economy—eco-

---

1. Conversation, Andries Waterboer, August 20, 1997.

2. Interview, Andries Waterboer, August 8, 1997.

nomic opportunities had been defined in terms of race. Within this grand scheme, Griqua people were largely uneducated coloreds and, as a result, *inkommers* occupied all positions of status and formal leadership. *Inkommers*, who had come to Griquatown for secure employment, were considered to be the educated elite, whereas *boorlings* saw themselves as "nothing people." The powerful *Kapteins* and prominent historical figures of the colonial period remained only in people's memories (Ross 1976). Their Griqua heritage had been largely dismissed by the Griquatown Council and by the apartheid government, which also manipulated their identity. In addition to classifying them as a subcategory of colored, it defined them in negative terms—as people not easily identified as either black or white. Left with few opportunities, *boorlings* were reduced to defining themselves in terms of place: of where they were from (or of origin) and of belonging (or birthright).[3] Place, then, provided a seemingly incontestable category whereby people were either born in Griquatown (or the surrounding area), and were therefore *boorlings*, or they were not. The *boorlings* were the people of historic Griquatown, the descendants of the *Kapteins* and of the extended families that surrounded and supported the *Kapteins*. They were, in other words, the progeny of the historical leaders who founded and shaped Griquatown. Although these inhabitants defined themselves in terms of place, they nonetheless spoke negatively of it. Griquatown was a depressed rural town often described as *vaal* (gray, bleak, and dismal). There was little to do in such a town and most people were anxious to leave and look for employment elsewhere. This ambiguity was expressed in terms of being Griqua—a heritage of pride and place

---

3. Strathern's work in the Essex village, Elmdom, UK, demonstrates a similar sense of belonging for indigenous families who remained at the center of village life (1981).

combined with their negative racial classification and a reality of bleakness and futility.

Although employment opportunities for *boorlings* were limited to manual labor between 1950 and about 1990, this did not stop people pursuing other avenues. The search for greater meaning and social status is evident in Isak Greeff's story. Isak had been a clever child and a willing student whose education was limited by the racial policies of the apartheid government. He explained that his father's employer had instructed his father not to

> give me a high [good] education, because the school principal wanted me to . . . be educated further as he saw I was a clever child. . . . My father worked for two teachers and they said to him: no, he must not give me too good an education, I should only be able to write my name and ensure that I do not enter through the incorrect door. Yes, a person cannot imagine it. [Household survey No. 49, Isak Greeff, October 27, 1997]

His schooling cut short prematurely, Isak did a number of odd jobs before finally securing employment as a driver. After being severely injured on duty, he retired in 1987. Thereafter he received a disability grant that he supplemented by repairing cars in his back yard.

Isak also belonged to the GPO, an organization that campaigned for official state recognition of the Griqua and thus enabled *boorlings* to be organizational leaders and political intermediaries at rallies and meetings. During the 1970s and 1980s, men such as Isak Greeff, Paul Pienaar, Andries Sekuti, and Jeliko Teis were strongly associated with the organization. They were all local residents, *boorlings*, and their involvement stemmed from a concern that Griqua heritage and descent should be recognized.

During the apartheid years, the GPO aimed to achieve governmental recognition of a specifically Griqua ethnic identity. The organization was reserved for *boorlings* and, as such, it expressed an ethnic identity that was explicitly related to place. This meant that *inkommers* who considered themselves Griqua, but who grew up elsewhere in South Africa, were not generally accepted as members. For example, Eddie Fortuin—whose comment about *inkommers* causing tension and being enemies of the family opened this article—was thought of as an *inkommer*. This perception was reinforced by his socioeconomic status and employment: initially as a teacher and subsequently a wealthy general dealer. He was actively excluded from the GPO, and Griquatown *boorlings* refused to consider him to be Griqua, even though he tried repeatedly to persuade them otherwise.[4] *Inkommers* were thus acutely aware that they were not accepted into the GPO and often voiced feelings of marginalization by the Griqua community.[5]

Despite—or perhaps because of—this marginalization, *inkommers*, as school teachers, principals, shop owners, or clerks, looked down from their positions of financial and employment security on Griqua culture, which they saw as primitive. Therefore, in contrast to the *boorlings* who were initiating their daughters according to Griqua custom (see below), the *inkommers* were sending their children to school, to university, and were acquainting them with more privileged colored and white society values. *Inkommers*, in keeping with elites in other South African towns, developed "a petty bourgeois consciousness with an acceptance of Victorian notions of respectability, progress and individual upliftment through hard work" (Vail 1989, p. 10). Being Griqua, meanwhile, was to be associated with less civilized values. To be Griqua was to initiate girls who were poor, uneducated, darker-skinned, and with unruly hair (Waldman 1989). It was, in other words, to be less presentable to society

---

4. Interview, Eddie Fortuin and Erick Scholtz, August 20, 1997.
5. Conversation, Dominee David Isaks, August 16, 1997.

and to be more outmoded. Nonetheless, being members of the GPO and stressing their ethnic identity gave Griqua *boorlings* a sense of importance that was contrary to their daily experiences and emphasized their unique identity in relation to *inkommers*. Given this ambiguous nature of Griqua identity, it was perhaps not surprising that the GPO became unpopular after the end of apartheid. Men such as Isak Greeff resigned from the GPO in the early 1990s, possibly in anticipation of the new democratic era with its increased potential for personal development. Isak's personal rationale was his increasing commitment to Christianity:

> Isak Greeff decided, in the late 1980s, that he no longer wanted to "live in the old world," and that he wished to move away from his old habits of drinking, swearing and lying. Following the Bible's instructions to "go forth into the world and preach the gospel to sinners," he sought to commit himself to the Lord's work. In the early 1990s, he joined several different churches with established *pastoors* (pastors) and tried—always unsuccessfully—to work with them. The clashes between Isak and other church leaders were caused by his attempts to promote himself as a serious minister and thus to acquire a position of leadership. [Household survey No. 49, Isak Greeff, October 27, 1997]

Isak's life, as described thus far, concerned his search for a sense of self and a desperate need to escape his real world of violence, drinking, and "disabledness." In this regard Isak was no different from a number of other *boorlings* in Griquatown. His disillusion with the GPO occurred alongside a trend toward the increased predominance of Pentecostal churches in Griquatown. As the apartheid era ended, the poorer *boorlings* were attracted to these small, charismatic churches. Griquatown was not the only place to experience this flourishing of new churches and Elphick

(1997) argues that "by the 1990s few places in the world, apart from the United States, matched South Africa in the proliferation of Christian denominations and sects" (p. 7). In Griquatown, the *Twaalf Apostels* (Twelve Apostles), the Gospel Mission, the *Beukes Kerk* (named after its initiator and leader), the *Baptiste* (Baptists), St. Phillips, and many others, were established by 1997. The large number of churches and the small congregations made it possible for numerous men to become *pastoors*. Postapartheid South Africa was experiencing an auspicious moment, with the heady freedom of possibility, and a religious fervor gripped Griquatown. Isak Greeff, who was desperate to be a dedicated *pastoor*, asked for guidance from the Lord:

> Isak and his wife spent two weeks fasting and praying. In a dream, the Holy Father said to him, "Greeff, Greeff, move away from those people, they will kill you because of the gospel you preach on my behalf," and directed him towards the *Christelike Kerk* (International Fellowship of Christian Churches). Although this church comprised only white members, it eventually agreed to accept Isak and his followers. For a brief period, the congregation embraced white and Griqua worshippers and more accurately reflected the new democratic nation, but the whites slowly drifted away and Isak then became the *pastoor* of the *Christelike Kerk*. [Household survey No. 49, Isak Greeff, October 27, 1997]

Isak's legitimacy can be seen to come directly from God, who conveyed his commands through prayer and dreams. Although it was clear that Isak had wanted to be a *pastoor*, he became involved with the *Christelike Kerk* because of God's instructions. Isak's role in this church had its roots in a sense of duty to follow God's calling, rather than a sense of choice (cf. Weber 1968). In becoming a recognized *pastoor*, Isak finally had his own church in which he conducted lengthy and enthusiastic church services. He conformed to West's (1975) description of African Independent Church leaders: married, middle-aged, and "ordinary," experiencing the same lack of education and employment as the rest of the congregation. Nonetheless, his congregation listened attentively to his sermons and believed in his right to lead them. As Weber (1946; cited in Lindholm 1990) argues:

> Whatever the leader says, whatever he asks, is right, even if it is self-contradictory. It is right *because the leader has said it*. The basis of the leader's legitimacy is the immediate "recognition" of his miraculous quality, and the disciple is lost in complete devotion to the possessor of this quality. [p. 25, original emphasis]

Isak's personal experience with God provided him with legitimacy and enabled others to acknowledge him as their spiritual leader.[6] It also gave Isak significant status in the eyes of other *boorlings*, although *inkommers* continued to look down on these Pentecostal churches. Two strands of identity, namely Isak's Griquaness and his Christianity, were intertwined in his actions and merit further attention. As for his Griquaness, Isak was unemployed, disabled, and a recipient of a state maintenance grant. In Griquatown many *boorlings* were similarly crippled by extreme poverty, illiteracy, and massive unemployment, despite the transition from apartheid to a democratic government. Nonetheless, this shift in governance did provide new opportunities for the ambitious, but uneducated, *boorlings*. Isak, like other men who had previously been attracted to the GPO, took advantage of these opportunities and accepted new leadership roles. Isak became

6. In the eighteenth and early nineteenth century, Khoi people saw dreams as a means of communication with supernatural beings and a sign of a particular individual's powers (Elbourne and Ross 1997).

the chairman of the school board[7] and he immersed himself in the Good Hope Society, a funeral organization run almost entirely by women. Within this organization he was known as *oupa* (grandfather), and was spoken of as one of the *groot mense* or adults of the organization. These terms reflect not only his adult status within the organization and community, but also indicate people's respect for his wisdom and seniority. Most importantly, though, Isak considered himself a *boorling* of Griqualand West. Although he had been born in the neighboring town of Niekerkshoop, and might therefore under different circumstances have been seen as an *inkommer*, he experienced none of the antagonism other *inkommers* reported. He felt completely at home in Griquatown.[8] Indeed Isak, as a disabled, unemployed, and uneducated man, did not fit the category of *inkommer*, and in constructing himself as a *boorling* he was making himself a "man of the people" (West 1975, p. 55). Unable to assert his social status through a belief in his abilities or his own resources or through socioeconomic status, he was on a par—both culturally and socioeconomically—with other Griquatown residents.

As for Isak's Christianity, contrary to all *inkommers*, Isak sought esteem and social standing in his relations with God and with other *boorlings* in the town. It was they who believed his dreams and accepted him as God's messenger, thus allowing him to carry out God's instructions and be their leader. In using Christianity to define respectability, Isak was following a Griqua tradition established in the days of the LMS mission station. Referring to the Khoi (indigenous pastoralists) and slave antecedents of Griqua society, Elbourne and Ross (1997) show that Christian-

---

7. After 1994 the secondary school could no longer maintain its racial exclusion policy and keep nonwhite children from attending (conversation, Isak Greeff, August 20, 1997).

8. Household survey No. 49, Isak Greeff, October 27, 1997.

ity provided a means of gaining respectability and renewing any sense of "honor lost by servitude" in the days of the LMS. Thus "Christianization and the widespread adoption of new norms of respectability were, for some coloured groups, building blocks for the reinvention of community" (p. 50). If Christianity was an opiate for the repressed pastoralists of the nineteenth century, then Pentecostalism and charismatic beliefs performed a similar role in the late twentieth century. Anderson and Pillay (1997) similarly suggest that "South African Pentecostalism . . . has its roots in a marginalised and underprivileged society struggling to find dignity and identity" (p. 240).

Christianity—with its emphasis on nuclear households and private space—and *boorling* status thus helped men such as Isak Greeff and Andries Waterboer to establish themselves as significant individuals in relation to *inkommers*. As men, they derived a fair degree of status from their Griqua and Christian identities, and other residents of Griquatown, Griqua women, *boorlings*, and some *inkommers* respected them for their achievements. In the sphere of everyday relations, men in Griquatown thus commanded a degree of authority and eminence. In relation to women and ritual, however, things were not as straightforward, and men could not retain their normal privileged statuses.

MEN AS *INKOMMERS*: RELATIONS WITH GRIQUA WOMEN

Being Griqua, and the importance of an alternative set of values, was not only emphasized by men in Griquatown. For women, being Griqua came more naturally—more as something inborn—and they were therefore seldom identified as either *boorlings* or *inkommers*. Griqua women were, like their menfolk, illiterate, very poor, and with few opportunities to develop status and financial well-being. Although women were committed members of the charismatic churches, they were unable to become *pastoors* and thus could not enhance their position within society. Women, therefore, emphasized values different from men's *boorling* identity. Griqua women stressed the importance of their role within the house through drawing on several different traditions and ideologies: The practices of their Khoi or pastoral ancestors emphasized women's autonomy in large extended, ostensibly patriarchal, households (Barnard 1992). Missionary values from the early nineteenth century stressed the importance of nuclear households and private space. Apartheid housing policy and modern influences also located women firmly within a nuclear home, but in the process possibly undermined their traditional Khoi authority over a broader domain. Women, in their ritual actions, brought these different—and sometimes contradictory—elements together and emphasized their autonomy within both a metaphorical Griqua home and a nuclear household. However, as the following two examples make clear, they had very few resources and very little control over their homes in their everyday lives.

Liesbet Waterboer, as head of her household, complained bitterly about the impossibility of living in a two-room house with five adult sons. Liesbet shared the double bed in the front room with her elderly and bedridden mother. What little space remained was used to pack clothes and other items. The second room served both as a kitchen and as a seasonal bedroom because, on cold nights, her sons erected temporary beds there, except for one son who had built an outside shelter. In warmer weather, they slept on the verandah. They survived on Liesbet's mother's old-age pension, as no one was employed. The house was thus under-resourced and severely overpopulated. Several windows were broken; the kitchen had only a small stove and an old ramshackle table on which stood several old and misshapen pots. Liesbet's sons—who all drank heavily and often arrived home drunk—frequently undermined her authority.

Maria Pieterse, a ritual expert, experienced similar problems even though she lived alone in her two-room house. The bedroom was furnished with two beds and a cupboard, and the kitchen had an ancient set of shelves, a small table, and some decrepit chairs. Maria survived on her old-age pension and the occasional benefits derived from initiation (or *hokmeisie*) rituals and *mokwele* transactions (described below). Once a month, when she received her pension, Maria's grandchildren, nieces, and nephews resident in Griquatown came to stay until the money was spent. Similarly, her children, all of whom were heavy drinkers, periodically visited from Johannesburg and cajoled her to buy alcohol. When she refused, they stole her money and returned home drunk and abusive. As a result, Maria was often forced to leave the home she was ostensibly in charge of.

Liesbet Waterboer and Maria Pieterse were exceptional women and yet, at the same time, remarkably ordinary. They were ordinary in their poverty and their experiences of employment, pensions, and everyday struggles. They were exceptional, not only because of their strong personalities, but also because of their roles in Griquatown: Liesbet was descended from Nicolaas Waterboer II (mentioned above), and Maria initiated young Griqua girls. In the context of extreme poverty and the difficulties of making ends meet on a day-to-day basis, both women emphasized their Griqua identity. Unlike Maria, Liesbet had never been initiated. Instead, she, like Isak Greeff and Andries Waterboer, was concerned that her Griqua heritage be recognized; she commented, "According to tradition, I'm an important person. My grandfather is Nicolaas Waterboer" (she never used her married surname).[9] Liesbet was proud to be recognized as Griqua and when researchers or inter-

---

9. Conversation, Liesbet Waterboer, August 14, 1996.

ested persons inquired about Griqua activities, she was one of the people called upon to impart information. Photographs of such events were housed in the local museum and she often spoke about these experiences.[10] Maria Pieterse was regarded as one of the *groot ou vroue* (adult women) who knew about *geloof* (tradition) and could initiate young girls. As in the case of Isak Greeff, this status endorsed her seniority, respect, and wisdom in cultural practices. Contrary to Maria's daily situation, the initiation rituals overseen by her endorsed women's strategic position within the home and emphasized women's control. It is to the initiation ritual that we now turn.

In the *hokmeisie*, the girls' initiation ceremonies, a young girl was secluded inside the house for about two weeks before undergoing a series of purification rituals and finally being introduced to the *waterslang* (watersnake).[11] The initiation was intended to protect the girl in her adult life and to socialize her into a Griqua woman, a process that involved guarding her sexuality and preparing her for conjugal relations.[12] For this reason, the girl was ostensibly initiated when menstruation began. She was expected to inform her mother, who hung a curtain across the bedroom corner and placed a mattress inside for the initiate. During initiation strict seclusion between men and women was practiced, as it was uncontrolled—and therefore unsocialized—sexuality that posed a danger to the new initiate. As the initiate's sexuality, fertility, and general well-being were at risk, it was imperative that only women occupy the house. The young initiate, secluded in the innermost section of the house, was in the pro-

---

10. Conversation, Liesbet Waterboer, November 24, 1997.

11. This *waterslang* was said to be a very beautiful male snake with long eyelashes and gorgeous eyes. On its forehead was a bright shining spot (Waldman 1989).

12. See Hoernlé (1918) for an anthropological interpretation of *Nama* (Khoi) girls' initiation ritual.

cess of being initiated into a female center. During her initiation she was surrounded by other women who were, I would argue, central to a Griqua identity. Contact with all men, not only outsiders but also brothers, fathers, grandfathers, and uncles—in other words *boorlings* to her immediate family— posed an immediate threat. This emphasis on men as being particularly pollutive allowed women to prevent their husbands, lovers, sons, and brothers from entering the house throughout the initiation period. Although excluded from the house, men surrounded the women during initiation. All night, they hung around the house, warming their bodies on a large fire, playing music, chatting, and drinking. Occasionally they would venture into the kitchen to ask for something, but mostly they gathered in the garden. The men's presence formed a visible barrier around the house within which women, and the initiate in the delicate process of becoming a woman, formed the focal point of Griqua identity. This structural positioning of men, as outside the home, was appropriate because, whereas women were ideologically bound to the house, men were thought of as free, sexually unrestricted, and expected to act accordingly.[13]

In asserting their control within the initiate's home, the women were also claiming a ritual authority within a wider

---

13. Women were expected to remain at home and were said to be "like houses." This reference explicitly related to women's sexuality and fertility. If a woman were to have sex outside of the house, and if a pregnancy resulted, she would have to bring the consequences of her actions back to her home. A man was said to be "like a car," mobile, free to go anywhere and meet anyone, and his penis was thought to be a bird. This association between men's penises and birds referred not to their bringing food back to a nest, but to their mobility, their ability to "sneak in anywhere," to make acquaintances and to be "at home" wherever they went. (Conversations, Sophie Julies, December 21 and 24, 1997; Marie Gouws, January 14, 1998; Trooi Visser, January 19, 1998; Sophie Julies, January 19, 1998. Interviews, Maria Pieterse and Mietha Amos, January 19, 1998, and Jacoba Swartz, January 14, 1998.)

domain. All the women present were collectively endorsing their association with the house, or houses in general, and their ritual power over the men gathered around the initiate's house. The positioning of women inside the house, and men outside as a protective barrier, was especially pronounced the evening before the initiate was to be introduced to the *waterslang*. Women who had earlier proved that they were not menstruating and therefore not polluting to the initiate, congregated indoors to supervise the initiate's purification rituals. Here they consumed the meat of the sacrificial sheep (that no man could eat). The pelvis bone was removed whole and cooked separately. Five postmenopausal women ate the meat off the pelvis bone, taking care not to damage the bone. This ritual precaution was necessary to safeguard the girl's sexuality and fertility. All the women spent the night with the initiate, often falling asleep in crowded and uncomfortable positions.[14] The women's presence and solidarity offered support for the following morning when the initiate would be at her most vulnerable and would be introduced to the *waterslang*.

The initiate, secluded at the center of the house, was one of, and positioned with, the women who were situated at the heart of the collective Griqua identity. Only women who had been correctly socialized into being Griqua could occupy such a central position, and this meant that their sexuality had been carefully prepared through initiation. Boys were not initiated, and being Griqua was therefore something inherently and specifically female. For a young female initiate, her union to the *waterslang* was her marriage into being Griqua. The white dress worn by the initiate echoed the marriage dress, and the *buchu*

14. In pre-colonial Khoi society, women appear to have eaten only mutton (Elphick 1977) and the Griquatown associations between women and sheep in the 1980s and 1990s may stem from these early traditions.

(an aromatic herb) offered to a male watersnake emphasized her sexual attraction.[15] Two tortoise shells, symbolic of her sexuality and her vagina, were filled with *buchu* and attached to her dress, positioned carefully over her ovaries.[16] This *buchu* was sprinkled onto the water so that the *waterslang* might be alerted to the people's presence. The remains of the sacrificial sheep, including the pelvis bone and other "dirt" from the initiation, were then thrown into the spring. The sinking of the pelvis bone, which represented the initiate's reproductive functions, signified that the *waterslang* had accepted her. It was also important that the *waterslang* see the tortoises (both the shells on her dress and her vagina) and acknowledge the girl as a proper Griqua woman by "releasing" or splashing over her as the old women beat the water around her. Thus it was that, when the snake saw the tortoises of the initiate, he was symbolically entering her, or engaging in sexual relations with her, and, in so doing, entering the Griqua house. The watersnake acted as, and represented, an *inkommer* into the broader Griqua family. He was,

---

15. There were numerous associations between women, sexuality, and tortoises in Griquatown. *Buchu* from the initiate's tortoise shells was rubbed over the sacrificial sheep's sexual organs before it was slaughtered. It was placed on young boys' testicles as a ritual prevention of sexual diseases and on young girls' nipples. *Buchu* was also used to bathe the initiate before she was taken to the *waterslang* and to appease the *waterslang*. (Interview, Maria Pieterse and Mietha Amos, January 19, 1998).

16. This ideological link between women and houses was further reinforced by old women, who would point to an association between a woman's vagina and a tortoise, and by young men who referred to frigid women as "dead tortoises." In addition, to have sex with a woman was to "see her tortoise." The tortoise—an anomalous animal, thought of as slow moving and carrying its home on its back, coupled with the rather phallic action of its head—was particularly appropriate for bringing together the notions of home and illicit sexual activity. To engage in illicit sexual relations with a woman—to penetrate her vagina or to "see her tortoise"—was like the antisocial habit of entering a house without permission and through the wrong entrance.

according to Carstens (1975), like a wealthy lover, and men re-
sented him. Seeing the watersnake as an *inkommer* and as the first
love of all the women socialized into being Griqua suggests that
it was this union between the young initiate and the watersnake,
the very first *inkommer*, that made her fundamentally Griqua.

Older women, such as Maria Pieterse, attempted to remain
influential as they used ritual to reinforce their position within
the house and, in so doing, to emphasize their strategic positions
within Griqua society. The ritual distinguished and credited those
women who knew Griqua traditions and were empowered to work
with these potentially dangerous ideological forces, while simultaneously emphasizing the authority and status of all women.
As mentioned above, Maria Pieterse's involvement with the initiates thus granted her a certain amount of prestige while the
ritual endorsed women's general solidarity. She also received
the slaughtered sheep's skin as a token of appreciation, which
she generally sold for a small amount of money.

Once initiated, women did not remain tied to the watersnake
all their lives, and their betrothal ceremonies to real men also
provided ritualized statements about Griqua gender relations. At
the time of betrothal, a man was expected to provide a sheep,
known as the *mokwele* sheep, for his in-laws. The *mokwele* ritual, with
a young man as its central protagonist, acknowledged, in contrast
to the *hokmeisie*, the impossibility of ensuring that Griquatown girls
remained virgins until marriage. Having sexual intercourse prior
to the bestowal of *mokwele* was a transgression often symbolized
as an illegitimate entry into the woman's home. The transfer of
mokwele—after transgressions had occurred—legitimated sexual
relations between a man and a woman in their immediate families' eyes and in the broader Griqua domain.

Although necessary for attaining adulthood manliness and
meant to occur when a man asked to marry a woman, the timing of *mokwele* and marriage were often staggered for several

reasons: First, the ceremony involved the expensive purchase of a sheep (to ensure the success of the marriage), tea, coffee, sugar, brandy (to seal the agreement between in-laws), and a *tjalie* (a traditional Griqua cape worn by women).[17] Second, the man might wish to establish whether his marriage would work before investing in *mokwele*. Finally, despite expectations that young men should initiate *mokwele* transactions between respective families, they did not request that their families provide *mokwele*. Rather, in keeping with being young and modern, they and their partner agreed to marry and announced their engagement. The bride's mother, accompanied by Maria Pieterse or another old woman who initiated young girls, would then—contrary to tradition—begin discussions around the payment of *mokwele*. Complete *mokwele* transactions seldom occurred in Griquatown and many people felt that only the tea, coffee, sugar, brandy, and tjalie were important.[18]

Although many *mokwele* transactions were initiated and spearheaded by the few old women who oversaw girls' initiation in the 1990s, it was seldom completed to their satisfaction. When Maria Pieterse "gave away" her daughter in a *mokwele* ceremony, she threatened that the man in question would be fined a sum of money if no *mokwele* sheep was forthcoming. However, this was bravado on her part, as no *mokwele* sheep was slaughtered and no fine paid. Young men, of marriageable age or recently married, were reluctant to be involved in *mokwele* transactions. Their reluctance stemmed from the associated cost and from the ritual itself, which degraded the man who made the presentation. They left arrangements to old women, and, even though they sometimes provided the sheep, they did not play a cen-

---

17. Survey No. 3, Ragel van Wyk, October 6, 1997.
18. Survey No. 14, Jelico Teis, October 8, 1997.

tral role in *mokwele*. Whereas the *hokmeisie* symbolized the ritual marriage of a young girl to a male watersnake, the *mokwele* ceremony concerned a man's—more profane—marriage to her. The *hokmeisie* ceremony was filled with ritual danger and the threat of pollution. For its duration, the girl secluded in the house was the most important person in the ritual. In contrast, the young man was not confined during the *mokwele* celebrations; indeed, he appeared marginal to the negotiations that took place between the parents and the old women.

In the *hokmeisie* ritual, a sheep was sacrificed in the yard at night. Only women in close proximity to the initiate ate this meat and these ritual actions safeguarded the initiate's sexuality and fertility. In contrast, the *mokwele* sheep was slaughtered during the daytime and the ceremony took place in the yard. Various women prepared salads in the kitchen and chatted as people came and went. Everyone ate outside where there was informal segregation along gender lines. *Mokwele* held no danger for the protagonists, contained no ritualistic prohibitions, and was not as important as the *hokmeisie* ceremony. Whereas *hokmeisie* initiates received choice bits of meat from the sheep sacrificed for them, potential sons-in-law were not allowed to eat from the *mokwele* sheep that they provided.

This disregard for the *mokwele* pelvis bone could be traced to the delayed timing of the ritual. Whereas other South Africans, for example the Tswana, sealed marriage transactions with a *mokwele* sheep (Breutz 1963), Griquatown people saw *mokwele* as a payment for sexual transgressions or when a man crossed the door's threshold.[19] Sexual relations with a woman were thus tantamount to an illicit entry into the woman's home, as the man repeated the symbolic actions of the watersnake. Johannes Pieterse explained:

---

19. Survey No. 18, Japie Maarman, October 9, 1997.

The *mokwele* thing goes like this. If you are going to marry the woman, look this is before you give the *mokwele* sheep, then you must pay "the door." I paid 17 pounds. Now then, when I had my oldest child [before my marriage], they said I entered the door, but they were not actually talking about the door. They said, "Look, as you've done this and you haven't yet asked for the woman, look, you've come in the back, you've come in the back of the *kraal* [byre], you've broken the back of the *kraal*."[20]

This account indicates that the illegitimate entry into houses where women reside was symbolic of a transgression of sexual rights. The two actions were directly associated. In having sexual relations with a woman, her suitor was surreptitiously entering the house without permission, through the door used by family members. *Mokwele* was thus related to women's sexuality and childbirth, and parents' acceptance of *mokwele* acknowledged their daughters' sexual activity.

In contrast to the *hokmeisie* ritual that ensured the construction of a genuine Griqua woman who "married" the *waterslang*, the *mokwele* ceremony emphasized a more mixed and ambiguous nature of being Griqua. The *mokwele* ritual was thus symbolic of marriages between men—either Griqua *boorlings* or non-Griqua *inkommers*—and Griqua women. All husbands-to-be, regardless of their ethnic origins, were considered *inkommers* to the girl's family, and mothers-in-law, in insisting on the provision of *mokwele*, reinforced bridegrooms' outsider status. Sons-in-law, as men who had illicitly "entered the house," did not command much respect, and perhaps it was for this reason that the *mokwele* ceremony played down their importance. Furthermore, as *inkommers*, not much was expected of these men. *Inkommers* could not be relied on to do what

---

20. Survey No. 9, Johannes Pieterse, October 7, 1997.

sons would do. Griqua mothers-in-law resigned themselves to *inkommers* who could never meet their expectations and who would never be as hardworking or committed as sons born to their own homes. Ouma Jacoba explained that an "*inkommer* will never do what your own [son] used to do."[21] The men's awareness of themselves—and people's lack of expectation—was reflected in their lack of interest in *mokwele*, and, if persuaded to provide *mokwele*, in their nonparticipation during the ceremony.

The gifts most often provided were tea, coffee, sugar, brandy, and a *tjalie*. Given to the bride's mother, the *tjalie* symbolized the labor involved in bringing up a daughter. The tea, coffee, and sugar were necessary for establishing and maintaining social relations and for socializing. Many women in Griquatown spent a considerable part of each day visiting and drinking tea at their friends' houses. Tea was always offered to important guests, even if this meant sending a child to borrow milk or sugar.[22] Thus these domestic items symbolized not only the relationships being established between the *inkommer* and his in-laws, between his family and his bride's family, but also—and very importantly—the network of established kin and *boorling* relations within Griquatown.

The ideology of a widespread Griqua "family" is further hinted in the transfer of brandy. Considered the most crucial of all *mokwele* items, the brandy symbolized the acceptance of the bridegroom into the nuclear family although, as mentioned above, this acceptance was never unconditional. It was drunk by the young man's

---

21. Interview, Jacoba Swartz, January 14, 1998.

22. Tea, coffee, and sugar were, in the 1870s, crucial to any journeys done on horseback. Women would pack these provisions into the saddlebags while men prepared their horses (Halford 1949). This importance may have led to the significance of tea, coffee, and sugar in ritual journeys in Griquatown today. These commodities also enabled people to emphasize their hospitality and, in so doing, to increase their own standing (Ross 1976).

in-laws who, during the process of drinking this brandy, questioned the young couple and decided whether to sanction their marriage. Brandy was also consumed when Griquatown residents were being introduced to a newborn baby. Here the brandy symbolized the newborn's urine. As the baby was born in Griquatown, he or she was a *boorling* of the place who needed to be introduced to Griquatown society or to kin outside his or her nuclear household. In order for this to take place, the members of the overarching Griqua "family" gathered at the child's house and drank the newborn's urine. The act was one of extreme intimacy and—having drunk of the baby's urine—everyone present "knew" the child in a personal and familiar manner. The act was intended to bestow good fortune by installing the baby into his or her place in Griqua society. Similarly, the brandy that was drunk at the *mokwele*, although not referred to as urine, provided a means to "know" the young man.

In keeping with the idea of an inclusive Griqua home that extended beyond the physical structures of a house, most people constantly sent food to—or received it from—people in other households. As illustrated in Maria Pieterse's household, children were often dispersed within several households as resources, and material items and people moved from house to house. People would also visit one another when they were hungry and I often watched women feeding neighbors or sending food to other Griquatown residents. In addition, personal property was hard to define and people would frequently wear each other's clothes or take items from one other. Women's ritual assertion of the importance of a widespread Griqua "family," with women in charge of the homes, was thus reflected in their survival strategies and in the desperation with which they sought to feed, clothe, and house their children. In so doing, these rituals emphasized women's status and ritual authority, while downplaying men's role in Griquatown. In ritual, men were thought of as inconsequential to the home and were consigned to the category "outsider."

CONCLUSION: GENDERED RELATIONSHIPS IN GRIQUATOWN

This article began with a comment from a man, not born in Griquatown, but married to a woman from the town and deeply committed to his Griqua identity. Nonetheless, because he was not from the town, and because of his socioeconomic success, he was considered "an enemy" to the family. The family referred to here was not a nuclear family, but rather an overarching Griqua family of *boorlings*. These *boorlings* (and many *inkommers*) were all related to each other in complex and multiple ways that could not always be accurately traced, and people often commented that Griquatown was one extended family. This relationship between place, family, and ethnic identity was often commented upon in Griquatown. Within this vision of Griqua identity, there were three main sources of authenticity and Griqua pride. The first, descent from the *Kapteins*, was considered original or authentically Griqua. Andries Waterboer, Liesbet Waterboer, and many other lineage members drew on this ideology. The second, also considered authentic, was open only to initiated women. Maria Pieterse and other skilled initiators thus developed their status and esteem in relation to their autochthonous Griqua identity. The old women wished to insert themselves into this broader family. In their ritual reiteration of the importance of women, of home, and of community, they sought to remind the people of Griquatown of their autochthonous status and, in so doing, to mask their dispossession and poverty. The communal eating and solidarity of women attained during ritual presented an ideal in which they, as household heads, oversaw their daughters' personal well-being and ensured that no one went hungry. The third source, drawn upon by most Griqua men, was their *boorling* status.[23] Their position was similar to that of uninitiated women who were of Griquatown, but were not unambiguously Griqua. For these people, excluded from the more definitive categories of Griquaness, there were fewer avenues of status and personal advancement available to be pursued. Nevertheless, they were members of the all-embracing Griqua family based on the extended Khoi households of the past. Albeit not core members, they too could benefit from the assistance, solidarity, and kinship that Griqua people offered each other.

Ideas about extended families inherited from their Khoi ancestors, and encapsulated in the notion of *boorlings*, mixed uncomfortably with Christian concepts of private space and nuclear families. Thus not everyone endorsed this ideology all the time. As seen in the case of Isak Greeff, Pentecostal Christianity enabled individuals to establish themselves as significant beings within very small congregations and created the means whereby people could redefine and limit their "families." This was extremely important in an environment in which assistance to neighbors, friends, and other Griquatown residents defined as "family" was generally obligatory. With everyone in dire need, the charismatic churches offered a means of limiting social relations and reciprocal obligations. The very small congregations made it possible for individual members to be important and for a sense of community to develop among individuals. In Griquatown, intimate ingroup relations, an increased sense of security and approval, and a certain status or standing were apparent among Church members. These intimate relations were reinforced through the use of the terms *brother* for men and *sister* for women (cf. West 1975). Congregation members defined themselves in terms of kin, honesty, and

---

23. Interview, Jan Balie, D. T. Campbell, August 28, 1996.

respectability, and developed relations of goodwill and measured reciprocity. This Christian identity also made it possible for men to escape the ambiguity associated with their part *inkommer*, part *boorling* identity and for women, who had never been initiated, to gain some recognition and respect.

The Pentecostal Churches thus allowed individuals—especially those who became *pastoors*—to develop a sense of status and authority and a means of asserting an alternative value system. Through charismatic leadership, Isak Greeff furthered his personal ideals while simultaneously holding onto, and indeed accentuating, his Griqua identity. In establishing his *boorling* identity and becoming a *pastoor*, Isak asserted an alternative set of values to those accentuated by successful *inkommers* and to those initiated Griqua women reinforced during ritual. In his, and other *boorlings'* eyes, it was through these Christian and Griqua values that they wished their lives to be evaluated rather than in terms of women's more exclusivist Griqua ideology or in terms of the more materialistic socioeconomic standards usually applied to— and by—South African citizens.

REFERENCES

Anderson, A. H., and Pillay, G. J. (1997). The segregated spirit: the Pentecostals. In *Christianity in South Africa: A Political, Social and Cultural History*, ed. R. Elphick and R. Davenport. Cape Town: David Philip.

Barnard, A. (1992). *Hunters and Herders of Southern Africa: A Comparative Ethnography of the Khoisan Peoples*. Cambridge, England: Cambridge University Press.

Boonzaier, E. (1984). *Economic Differentiation and Racism in Namaqualand: A Case Study.* Second Carnegie Enquiry into Poverty and Development in Southern Africa, conference paper No. 68. Cape Town: University of Cape Town.

Breutz, P. L. (1963). *The Tribes of the Districts of Kuruman and Postmasburg.* Ethnological publications No. 49. Pretoria: The Government Printer.

Carstens, P. (1975). *Some Implications of Change in Khoikhoi Supernatural Beliefs.* In *Religion and Social Change in Southern Africa: Anthropological Essays in Honour of Monica Wilson*, ed. M. G. Whisson and M. West. Cape Town: David Philip.

Elbourne, E., and Ross, R. (1997). Combating spiritual and social bondage: early missions in the Cape Colony. In *Christianity in South Africa: A Political, Social and Cultural History*, ed. R. Elphick and R. Davenport. Cape Town: David Philip.

Elphick, R. (1977). *Kraal and Castle: Khoikhoi and the Founding of White South Africa.* London: Yale University Press.

——— (1997). Introduction: Christianity in South African history. In *Christianity in South Africa: A Political, Social and Cultural History*, ed. R. Elphick and R. Davenport. Cape Town: David Philip.

Halford, S. J. (1949). *The Griquas of Griqualand: A Historical Narrative of the Griqua People. Their Rise, Progress, and Decline.* Cape Town: Juta.

Hoernlé, A. W. (1918). Certain rites of transition and the conception of !Nau among the Hottentots. *Harvard African Studies* 2:65–82.

Lindholm, C. (1990). *Charisma.* Cambridge, England: Basil Blackwell.

Pearson, P. (1986). The history and social structure of the Rehoboth Baster community of Namibia. Unpublished MA thesis, University of the Witwatersrand, Johannesburg, South Africa.

Ross, R. (1976). *Adam Kok's Griqua.* Cambridge, England: Cambridge University Press.

Strathern, M. (1992). *After Nature: English Kinship in the Late Twentieth Century.* Cambridge, England: University of Cambridge Press.

Vail, L. (1989). Introduction. In *The Creation of Tribalism in Southern Africa*, ed. L. Vail. London: James Currey.

Waldman, P. L. (1989). Watersnakes and women: a study of ritual and ethnicity in Griquatown. Unpublished BA (honors) dissertation, University of the Witwatersrand, Johannesburg, South Africa.

——— (2001). The Griqua conundrum: political and socio-cultural identity in the Northern Cape, South Africa. Unpublished Ph.D. dissertation, University of the Witwatersrand, Johannesburg, South Africa.

Weber, M. (1968). *Max Weber on Charisma and Institution Building*. Chicago: University of Chicago Press.

West, M. (1971). *Divided Community: A Study of Social Groups and Racial Attitudes in a South African Town*. Cape Town: Balkema.

——— (1975). *Bishops and Prophets in a Black City: African Independent Churches in Soweto*. Johannesburg, Cape Town: David Philip.

from *America*

GENDER IN AMERICA

―――

Drucilla Cornell

IN THE UNITED STATES, the first great wave of feminism—the feminism that grew out of the abolitionist movement to rid U.S. society of slavery—did not explicitly develop a concept of gender. Rather, its position was that all forms of inequality should be eradicated—even those that implied biological difference—because these differences should not be relevant to political citizenship. Some of the abolitionist feminists remained true to their program of radically antihierarchical egalitarianism (Richards 1993), even as their movement came to be identified with two white leaders: Elizabeth Cady Stanton and Susan B. Anthony (Davis 1982), both of whom supported one major issue—women's suffrage—as crucial to the resolution of other forms of inequality that plagued women's lives in the nineteenth and early twentieth century. Stanton, in particular, used sexual difference as a justification for giving women the right to vote: women, she argued, would bring their civilizing role in the home into the public arena. Unfortunately, she abandoned her abolitionist roots in the process; she argued that granting white middle-class women the right to vote would help them achieve equality with the white male majority, thereby extricating them from the position of being merely equal to immigrants, blacks, and other poor minorities. With the passage of the right to vote in 1920, first-wave feminists focused their political and legal efforts on the passage of an Equal Rights Amendment (ERA). Union organizers and others opposed the ERA for its potential to erode the minimum protective rights that had been guaranteed to some women workers. This class-based dispute was never fully resolved, and it led to the failure of the ERA and of the first wave of feminism itself. (Incidentally, I first heard of the word *feminist* and indeed *lesbian* when both were applied to my grandmother, who owned a major printing company at a time when no other women did. [Cornell 2002]. When I asked my grandmother whether she was either a feminist or a lesbian, she replied, "Not really, but of course I think women are equal to men.")

From its very inception, the second wave of feminism introduced the idea of gender roles—an idea largely borrowed from modern social theory. Indeed, it was the challenge to those roles that inspired many women—including myself—to become feminists. One of the major ways in which women of my generation—particularly white Anglo women who were citizens of the United States—came together was through consciousness-raising groups. The basic idea behind such groups was that, through the elaboration of each other's stories, we could see how we had been forced into gender roles—the first step to rebelling against them. This kind of feminist activism and organizing was crucial as even in the civil rights, black power, and student movements of the 1960s, women often found themselves filling traditional roles of what women were supposed to do: they made coffee, they encouraged their men, they did the office work. The way women were treated exposed the hypocritical sexism behind the call for radical equality and freedom of oppressed peoples. In my own case, I first announced myself as a feminist when a young man in my Students for a Democratic Society (SDS) group announced that I had a political obligation to sleep with him. For "feminist" reasons, I said no. From that moment on, I identified myself as a feminist. But like many of my generation, it has been a long struggle to come to terms with what feminism is and, more specifically, how it defines its own relationship to gender.

Gender as an analytic category was the creation of second-wave feminism, which came to dispute openly the idea that biological difference between the sexes should ever be used—even affirmatively—to justify women's participation as citizens. Since the second wave of feminism, feminists have militated against the idea that anatomy is destiny. The need to grasp how exactly women become women led feminists to introduce the category of gender. Differences once considered entirely biological and bodily came to be seen as socially constructed during the long historical division of the human race into men and women. Viewed as a set of reified meanings, imposed stereotypes, and internalized roles that force us to be on one side or the other of this divide, gender quickly gained enormous explanatory power. The early use of gender was often critical; it was used to expose lacunae in literary, social, political, and scientific work, and to show that any history told without gender missed the crucial developments and struggles various literary texts, social movements, political institutions, and scientific discoveries were trying to elaborate. History is formed through its own gendered formation: this became the new watchword. In many different disciplines, and in rather novel ways, gender illuminated how women were oppressed to a degree that had never before been given credence: how women played a more significant role in social, political, and economic life than had previously been recognized by dominant modes of historiography. Feminists realized they had to challenge the resolute division within classical liberal political philosophy between the public and private spheres. For it rendered women's work invisible in the domestic sphere—work that allowed men to seek employment outside the home—and considered productive labor to be exclusively market-driven.

Despite all this, the critical use of gender was fraught with analytic tension. As a category of analysis, gender illuminated the social construction of the various differences that brought about a great divide between sexed beings. Yet even though it did not necessarily have to focus on women, gender was analytically deployed during the second wave to create a social identity for all women. Gender could function as the ultimate ground of feminist analysis and critique. It was precisely this deployment of gender that women of color called into question. They argued strongly that their interests, their identifications, and their positions had not been adequately represented due to the complicity of white women in structural racism and inequality. In a rightfully well-known article, Kimberlé Williams Crenshaw (1991) introduced the idea of intersectionality to demonstrate how race, class, and gender are all part of how black women lived both their blackness and their womanhood, and how they are discriminated against in society through the intersections of these three forms of oppression. As a theoretical as well as philosophical matter, intersectionality demanded that feminists expand the very analyticity of gender; it could no longer be legitimately used to name a social identity. It ceased being sui generis as a category of analysis; it had to be seen as intersecting with other categories of analysis.

A no less important theoretical and philosophical challenge to gender came from Judith Butler (1990). She argued that it is a mistake to treat gender as a self-consistent category since that forces feminists to ontologize what it is to be a man or woman, as if these meanings were somehow the result of a prior way of being in the world. "If one 'is' a woman," Butler famously writes in *Gender Trouble*, echoing Crenshaw,

> that is surely not all one is; the term fails to be exhaustive, not because a pre-gendered "person" transcends the specific paraphernalia of its gender, but because gender is not always constituted coherently or consistently in different historical contexts, and because gender intersects with racial, class, ethnic, sexual, and regional modalities of discursively constituted identities. As a result, it becomes impossible to separate out "gender" from the political and cultural intersections in which it is invariably produced and maintained. [p. 3]

Butler's radical assertion is that "woman" does not denote a common identity and, even more radically, that it is ethically and politically undesirable for feminism to seek in the category of woman a universal basis for its ethics and politics. She deepens Crenshaw's idea of intersectionality by pointing out that, when it is universalized, the concept of woman cannot but privilege hegemonic Western ideas concerning gender and women's oppression. Butler pushes our thinking toward the "regional modalities of discursively constituted identities" and thus away from a "global subject" that endlessly implicates us in our Western imperialist past. "The critical task for feminism," she tells us at the end of *Gender Trouble*,

> is not to establish a point of view outside of constructed identities; that conceit is the construction of an epistemological model that would disavow its own cultural location and, hence, promote itself a global subject, a position that deploys precisely the imperialist strategies that feminism ought to criticize. The

critical task is, rather, to locate strategies of subversive repetition enabled by those constructions, to affirm the local possibilities of intervention through participating in precisely those practices of repetition that constitute identity and, therefore, present the immanent possibility of contesting them. [p. 147]

Butler's emphasis on the regional discursive constitution of women does not lead us simply to examine its ethically suspicious underpinnings; it forces us to recognize the moral injunction of heterosexual normativity that has been integral to our very conceptualization of women. Butler's crucial insight is that gender itself is a form of repetition of imposed norms that decide not only how our bodies come to matter, but also how they are given meaning and gendered, and, moreover, how we are enjoined to love only members of the "opposite sex." In Butler's account, the delimitation of gender as a coherent social identity for women is heterosexist since it at once excludes certain marginalized populations—gays, lesbians, transsexuals, and the transgendered—and reinscribes their exclusion at the margins of society.

The fact that gender was incorporated into the U.S. legal system is the result of this heterosexism being given the imprimatur of law. Under Title VII of the Civil Rights Act (1964), discrimination is not allowed on the basis of "sex." But the lawyers who bravely took up the initial cases of sex discrimination made a not-so-brave decision to interpret sex as gender. As a result of how gender was defined legally, gays and lesbians, transsexuals, and the transgendered were left beyond the reach of formal legal equality. A claim of gender discrimination had to show (1) that an individual woman or a group of women were discriminated against by an employer or a policy, or (2) that they were similarly situated to a group of men and yet treated differently from them. The question immediately arose: What did it mean to be discriminated against as a woman?

To proceed through the gender comparison model provided by formal legal equality, a claim of discrimination thus had to show that a characteristic is universal to women and, at the same time, not unique to them so that there could be a basis of comparison of women with men. Where there is no basis of comparison with men, no legal discrimination can be found, and when the characteristic is not universal to women, then there is no comparison between women and men because said comparison would only be within that class of women (Cornell 1995).

The unwavering rejection of sexual difference as legally relevant led feminists to waver before the issue of pregnancy. Hence the frenzied search to find ways to argue that pregnancy was analogous to some engendered condition in men. The analogies never seemed to work. The underlying problem was that the measure for equality being used was modeled on the masculine subject in the guise of the person. To demonstrate their equality, women had to show that they were identical to men at least in those properties relevant for the challenged classification. When it came to pregnancy, such a showing seemed impossible to make. In a now infamous Supreme Court decision, *Geduldig v. Aiello*, Justice William H. Rehnquist rejected a challenge to an insurance policy that covered male-related disorders but not pregnancy because under his analysis the refusal of coverage was due to a real difference that insurance companies could rationally take into account, particularly since it only affected disadvantaged pregnant women and not all women. Writing for the Court, Rehnquist claimed that normal pregnancy

is an objectively identifiable physical condition with unique characteristics. Absent a showing that distinctions involving pregnancy are mere pretexts designed to effect an invidious discrimination against the members of one sex or the other, law-makers are constitutionally free to include or exclude pregnancy from the coverage of legislation such as this on any reasonable basis, just as with respect to any other physical condition. [cited in Cornell 1995, p. 62]

His argument was not only that there was no invidious discrimination, but also that pregnancy was a unique physical condition that differentiated women from men. Yet the real problem in *Geduldig* did not stem in any way from the condition per se, but from the evaluation of the insurance companies that did not find pregnancy worth covering. The problem was with the evaluation, not with the purported difference. This is a classic example of how the devaluation of the feminine is attributed to nature, to a natural difference. But nature does not make evaluations— human beings do.

Surprisingly, Congress acted to overturn Rehnquist's decision and argued against an intraclass distinction between pregnant and nonpregnant persons by insisting that pregnancy could be identified in some way with women. The question of what the discrimination of women meant legally was thereby left unsuccessfully answered; the concept of equality underwriting the law was too formalistic: like should be treated alike. It assumed that women were like men in terms of social and economic positioning, cultural training, and in their actual employment situations. What happens to the oppression of women? Does not such oppression put women in a position that can never be that of similarly situated men? The conservative answers to these questions held constant class hierarchies, gender stereotypes, and racist assumptions. In her pathbreaking legal analysis, Catherine Mackinnon argued that women's oppression consisted in the socially constructed reality that they could never be similarly situated to men. Mackinnon's (1979) early attempts to define sexual harassment as discrimination against women failed because of the simple fact that not all women are sexually harassed, whereas some men are. Under formal legal equality, therefore, she had no defensible claim. Still, she defended the idea that

> practices which express and reinforce the social inequality of women to men are clear cases of sex-based discrimination in the inequality approach. Sexual harassment of working women is argued to be employment discrimination based on gender where gender is defined as the social meaning of sexual biology. Women are sexually harassed by men because they are women, that is, because of the social meaning of female sexuality, here, in the employment context. Three kinds of arguments support and illustrate this position: first, the exchange of sex for survival has historically assured women's economic dependence and inferiority as well as sexual availability to men. Second, sexual harassment expresses the male sex-role pattern of coercive sexual initiation toward women, often in vicious and unwanted ways. Third, women's sexuality largely defines women as women in this society, so violations of it are abuses of women as women. [p. 174]

Mackinnon felt that it is precisely because women are the sexually harassed that they can never be men's equals in this society. For her, the paradox of gender was that it was ultimately reducible to women's sexual role within heterosexuality. To be a woman, to be engendered as a woman, meant to be available at all times for men's pleasure, manipulation, and control. Although no court ended up accepting Mackinnon's analysis of how gender and having a woman's sex were integrally connected, several of the U.S. circuit courts tried to turn her position—that until women were freed of certain forms of male behavior they could not be the equals of men—into a defensible legal claim of equality. Some courts argued that a woman's viewpoint, even if it

seemed abstract and unreasonable, should be a key factor in determining what constituted an act of sexual harassment. In the early
1980s, this legal position was informed by the work of Carol
Gilligan (1982), who, like Mackinnon and other second-wave
feminists, accepted the idea that gender is socially constructed. But
socially constructed or not, Gilligan thought the engendering of
women through their roles in the family could lead them to develop what she called a different voice. Gilligan was misunderstood to argue that there is a statistically demonstrable correlation
between this voice and all women. Her point was more general:
in the interviews she conducted, more women than men seemed
to embrace an ethic of care, and that this ethic should be taken
seriously and placed alongside a certain conception of justice.
Mackinnon militantly disagreed not only with Gilligan but also
with the view of gender discrimination that tried to correct the
failures of formal legal equality by introducing a different voice.
That women were engendered to have a different voice was, for
Mackinnon, part of the problem, not the solution.

Like the first wave, the second wave of feminism tried to pass
into law an equal rights amendment. Once again it was defeated,
but some arguments around protective legislation were introduced, and unions and certain women's groups supported the
amendment anyway. In keeping with the idea that gender roles
should not be allowed to determine women's fate, Mackinnon
actually felt at least one of the reasons for the failure of the passage of the second ERA was the acceptance of women in their
supposed difference. She attacked Gilligan in particular for per-
petuating that difference, even despite the fact that, as I have
suggested, Gilligan's own argument was never meant to support such a perpetuation. Ironically, Mackinnon's own analysis
of gender as socially constructed through the engendering of
women as a sex led her to reject the idea that gender needed to
be intersected with other categories of analysis in order to make

sense of women's actual positions in society and under law. Her early work on sexual harassment as a symptom of how women are engendered as a sex led her to antipornography legal activism. Porn for the later Mackinnon is perhaps the ultimate symptom of what it means for women to be the sex for men. Feminists within legal institutions and those outside them sparred over Mackinnon's attempts to introduce into law a civil ordinance that, in the name of gender equality, would regulate the distribution of porn and hence its effects in promoting the inequality of women. Mackinnon sincerely believes there is such a thing as a gender identity for women. The difference in women's oppression is simply a matter of degree not of kind. As a result, she feels she can legitimately make generalizations about what women's position is as a gender in society and thus what substantive equality requires. But if there is no place for a different voice of gender in Mackinnon's work because it is simply the rattling of women's chains, then there is by extension no place for differences between women based on race, class, ethnicity, and language. Since we are all constructed under the hegemony of heterosexuality, there is also no real lesbianism or gayness. In fact, in the ordinance advocated by Mackinnon and her colleague, Andrea Dworkin, gay men and transsexuals can sue only if they are positioned as women for the purposes of the harms imposed by pornography. Although the ordinance is written in the language of subordination of women, Mackinnon and Dworkin hold out the possibility that gay men and transsexuals, if positioned as "fuckees," may thus be positioned as women for purposes of showing harm under the ordinance. Ultimately, despite all Mackinnon's differences with formal equality theorists, she shares a certain problem with them: she ends up speaking about all women without any recognition of the privileges and differences between them. All women in this way are subsumed under a social as well as legal category of analysis that cannot even make sense of a black woman, let alone other women of color.

Under our constitution, race is a suspect classification because it is purportedly an unchanging characteristic, and sex is classified at an intermediate level of judicial scrutiny. But what about discrimination against a group of black women or an individual black woman? To decide which level of judicial scrutiny black women should be given, a few initial questions had to be asked: How black is a black woman? How much of a woman is she? Is a black woman one-half woman, one-third woman, or two-thirds black? How these questions were answered had serious legal consequences. The deeper problem that many critical race theorists saw was that the gendered figure of woman introduced into the law was thoroughly whitened (Austin 1989, Caldwell 1991). The rejection by an employer of any form of cultural affirmation of blackness was therefore seen as nondiscrimination. Women who tried to sue because they had been fired or harassed for braiding or locking their hair were denied legal standing because hairstyle was considered neither an immutable characteristic nor an essential attribute of womanhood. Other women of color had similar problems, although they were not identical: Hispanics and Latinas were considered white, and so their color was not considered an immutable characteristic. In this way, sexual minorities, black women, and women of color have all found themselves unable to translate their own experience of discrimination into a legal claim of redress. The upshot is that relatively few women have benefited from gender becoming a codified legal category.

Within our legal system, we must introduce the moral and legal ideal of the imaginary domain in order to address all of the above challenges to gender. As I have defined it within the legal sphere, the imaginary domain is the moral and psychic right to represent and articulate the meaning of our desire and our sexuality within the ethical framework of respect for the dignity of all others. This domain is imaginary in the sense that it is irreducible to actual space. But it is also imaginary in a psychoanalytic sense. Our assumed identities have an imaginary dimension since they are shaped through our identification with primordial others. Without these identities, we cannot envision who we are. Our identifications with others as they have imagined and continue to imagine us form our self-image. These identifications color the way in which we envision ourselves, but they do not determine the reach of our imagination in dreaming up who else we might be. In this way, we can distinguish the imaginary from the radical imagination in which we envision new worlds and configure what has otherwise remained invisible. The radical imagination demands some degree of psychic separation. Otherwise our dreams of who we might become, both individually and collectively, would be captured by unconscious claims on us.

We are all born in a given body. We all have deep and profound sexual desires that often guide us rather than the other way around. Feminists have critiqued the legal concept of the person because it does not capture our concrete reality as embodied human beings with an irreducible particularity of bodily as well as sexual experience. Yet normatively speaking, we should not want law to address that particularity. Instead, as a matter of right, the law ought to protect us as the creative sexual beings we are. All human beings mark their sexual differentiation from each other, but not in the same way. In view of this incontrovertible fact, a rigid ontology of sexual differentiation makes little sense. We should thus be able to represent and freely play with how we live out our lives as sexually differentiated beings in no way fated to be masculine or feminine. Freedom is the right to represent who we are sexually. It can be limited only by representations of sexual difference that fundamentally degrade others in the exercise of their same freedom. We must, then, shift the category of comparison from actual men to an ideal of the person that functions as the universal legal standard according to which our freedom and equality as free and equal persons become possible.

Why have I focused so much on the ways in which gender has been translated into the law? In the United States, the idea that law is the defining category of theoretical as well as practical analysis reaches far beyond those who are legal professionals. Indeed, it is the very codification of gender that continues to define and limit it analytically. Any thought of the return to sexual difference, let alone feminine sexual difference, is thus seen as a regression to a prefeminist theory of anatomy as destiny. This is in large part because of how feminists have tried to turn gender into an actually existing identity rather than focus on men and women's complex identification with sex and gender positions—the fact that these positions can never fully capture the uniqueness or the complexity of such identifications. My own understanding of the imaginary domain focuses on the freedom law must give to each one of us to reimagine and resymbolize for ourselves the meaning of both sex and gender identifications. Since within psychoanalytic theory identifications have a subjective component and an imaginary aspect, they are always fluid and thus not easily captured by designated identities. Through the use of psychoanalytic theory, we can problematize gender identity in such a way that does not deny there is a demand of our embodied being that must be addressed as our sexual difference. For it allows us to claim, with full logical consistency, that no one is simply a woman or captured in the identity of women, and at the same time that feminine sexual difference is infinitely representable since it is brought into being through sexual differentiation between human beings. Only psychoanalysis can completely return sexual difference to gender analysis and further Simone de Beauvoir's (1953) insight that one is not born a woman, but becomes one—the insight that was the beginning of our understanding of the social construction of gender. Some feminists think the fluidity of our identifications, when considered alongside the conservative uses of gender as a social and legal category of analysis, necessarily leads to the conclusion that we should no longer deploy gender as a critical concept or category. But others have concluded—and I am among them—that there are entrenched positions and sedimented meanings of the masculine and feminine that continue to be foisted on men and women, and that they can be traced in various forms of social scientific analysis, even if that analysis remains subject to different interpretations. In one way or another, these positions and meanings must be connected to what Butler rightly describes as the hegemonic normativity of heterosexuality.

In the United States, it was only after the famous Stonewall riots in New York City in 1969 that the proclamation that one is gay or lesbian became as much a matter of ethical and political significance as of personal self-definition. To be sure, some courageous souls have always been open as gays and lesbians, particularly in downtown Manhattan. But the bars and clubs there are often places where people hide out from public lives that demand they be straight in their day-to-day functioning in society. Still, after Stonewall, the movement for gay and lesbian rights became both open and militant, leading to fundamental social and legal challenges to the inequality of people who lived outside the norms of heterosexuality. Although these advances are now being challenged under the conservative presidency of George W. Bush, gays and lesbians have won for themselves—at least in some states in the United States—something like parity with heterosexuals. Yet the very notion of parity implies that normative heterosexuality is still very much in place, and that gay and lesbian legal claims of access to certain insurance and health-care benefits are determined by the heterosexism built into the law. Gays and lesbians can appear to have rights only so long as they conform to gender stereotypes thoroughly buttressed by heterosexual normativity. The problem of how to protect the rights of gays and lesbians under the law becomes even more problematic under the formal legal equality theory of gender analysis.

Sexual orientation is usually seen as a choice, even if an unconsciously imposed one, that cannot be understood as being similar to purportedly immutable characteristics such as race and biological difference between the sexes. But the gay and lesbian movement challenged both the social and legal meaning that had been given to gender, arguing that gender could be separated from sexual orientation and the way one lives out one's sexuality. Indeed, the development of queer theory and queer activism was inseparable from many gay and lesbian activists' rejection of gender equality as inherently conservative, whether interpreted as substantive equality, formal legal equality, or as a means of comparison between actually existing men and women. As many feminists understand it, equality turns on the comparison of one identifiable group with another identifiable group. Queer theorists argue instead that freedom from such identities and how that freedom becomes possible must be the basis for any analysis of how we are imprisoned by the category of gender and how we might re-create ourselves so as to free ourselves from the identitarian sameness that inheres in both feminist and liberal conceptions of equality. The most searching critique from queer theorists is that as long as feminists remain committed to gender equality, we remain captured by the very identities that force us into a kind of determined self-definition. At its most radical, queer theory emphasizes the need for self-creation and its ethical movement beyond the categories of any already established identity. Hence Michael Warner's (2000) provocative interrogative gesture, and his answers:

> What identity encompasses queer girls who fuck queer boys with strap-ons, or FTMs (female-to-male transsexuals) who think of themselves as queer, FTMs who think of themselves as straights, or FTMs for whom life is a project of transition and

screw the categories anyway? . . . Criticisms once confined to
queer theory can now be lived out and expressed in politics. . . .
Alterity poses a deeper challenge than mere diversity. It requires
a culture of encounter, a space for transformation that doesn't
specify everyone's identity in advance.

Of course, there has always been a strand of feminist theory in
both the first and second waves of feminism interested in experiments in living and in freedom, over and against the struggle to
achieve gender equality. Indeed, this has brought some feminists
closer to queer theory and the project of developing an ethics of
freer, more experimental living. The ubiquitous Martha Nussbaum
(2000) is one such feminist. In a recent essay on Michael Warner's
work, she had no qualms admitting that

every society has its chosen "shameful" and "disgusting" sexual
minorities who come to represent properties—stickiness, fluidity,
sheer corporeality—that the dominant group would like to forget
that it, too, possesses. Women play this role in more or less all
cultures. But Warner is surely right in suggesting that this powerful emotional reaction to one's own perceived incomplete-
ness is behind the virulence of much American homophobia,
particularly when directed against gay men. . . . If we cannot
dissociate ourselves from our patterns of desire and approval,
including our desire to conform—and Warner knows that for
the most part we cannot—we can at least think, and we can at
least criticize, rather than just falling mindlessly back on the
old ways and scorning those who are different. . . . We call
shame and disgust to our aid when we want to avoid looking
seriously into our own sexual lives; and so the politics of shame
is also the refusal of serious self-scrutiny. This invitation to
thought, to the examined life, is the most attractive proposal,
and the most challenging, indecent proposal, that queer cul-

ture makes to American democracy. They say to you, be someone else. I say: believe them.

One question that arises, though, for both feminists and
queer theorists is, What does this queer ethics of living and
thinking mean for an inevitably embodied and sexually alive
creature? The recent work of the transgendered to claim their
rights to social support for hormonal treatment and medical
operations raises the question of gender in an emergent
ethical as well as political context. Ironically, the procedures
in place in most of the United States today assume gender stereotypes as the basis for a psychiatric judgment of whether a
person who seeks the body of the other sex can actually have
an operation, let alone seek social support for it. For instance,
some states that do allow the possibility of socially supported
hormonal treatment and operations insist that, after hormonal
treatment, the individual involved show that he or she can
successfully fit into society as a traditionally defined male or
female. Due to the way in which the transgendered have been
forced to conform to these regulations, some gay, lesbian, and
transgender activists have even questioned whether the desire
to achieve the body of the other sex is not inherently conservative by reinforcing gender stereotypes and the normalcy of
heterosexuality. In other words, one can truly love a woman
only if one is in the position of a man, if one is a man seeking
to achieve a woman's body. Butch lesbians in particular have
argued that some "tranny girls" (transsexuals) are actually
running away from their own butchness by seeking conformity with traditional gender roles. But again, psychoanalysis
has put into question whether the force of sexual difference—
when expressed in the desire to be a different body—can or
should be reduced to even the most sophisticated theories of
the social construction of gender.

How does a woman end up in a man's body? And what is the relationship between an understanding of feminine sexual difference as infinitely expressible and the desire to transform the body in accordance with the identification "I am a woman in the wrong body" or "I am a man in the wrong body"? The figure of the transgendered demands that we look more deeply at the relationships among gender, sexual difference, and sexual orientation as they have been currently defined. In different ways, queer theory, queer activism, and the recent struggles of the transgendered have both challenged and provoked new thinking about the relationships among sex, sexual difference, and gender. Although some feminists have now become convinced that queer theorists are right to find gender inadequate or conservative, not only in law but more generally as a critical category of analysis, the transgendered have reminded us that we cannot so easily dispense with the idea of gender. Perhaps there is a deeper theoretical point to be made here: since gender was developed in the political context of feminism, and since its meaning has shifted as feminists have challenged the various meanings that gender has been given within feminist theory, gender itself as a category is inseparable from its deployment by political movements. The future of gender, then, is not simply a theoretical question. As the transgendered have brought their demands into the political arena, they have shown us that gender can be deepened and rethought as much as it can be challenged as a category. The future of gender as a category of analysis will continue to be bound up with the politics surrounding its use and analytic efficacy. At times, this analytical politics has transformed gender into a thoroughly divisive category, as in the case of formal equality analysis and Mackinnon's own conception of substantive gender equality. Yet at other times, it has allowed us to see the relations among corporeal givenness, sexual difference, and the engendering of our bodies. Does gender have a future in the United States? The answer to that question awaits the movements that will deploy it, challenge it, and, it is hoped, rearticulate its meaning.

REFERENCES

Austin, R. (1989). Sapphire bound! *Wisconsin Law Review* 1989(3).

Butler, J. (1990). *Gender Trouble*. New York: Routledge.

Caldwell, P. (1991). A hair piece: perspectives on the intersection of race and gender. *Duke Law Journal* 41(397).

Cornell, D. (1995). *The Imaginary Domain: Abortion, Pornography and Sexual Harassment*. London: Routledge.

——— (2002). *Between Women and Generations: Legacies of Dignity*. New York: St. Martin's Press.

Crenshaw, K. W. (1991). Mapping the margins: intersectionality, identity politics and violence against women of color. *Stanford Law Review* 43.

Davis, A. (1982). *Women, Race, and Class*. New York: Random House.

de Beauvoir, S. (1953). *The Second Sex*, trans. and ed. H. M. Parshley. New York: Alfred A. Knopf.

Gilligan, C. (1982). *In a Different Voice: Psychological Theory and Women's Development*. Cambridge, MA: Harvard University Press.

Mackinnon, C. (1979). *Sexual Harassment of Working Women*. New Haven, CT: Yale University Press.

Nussbaum, M. (2000). Experiments in living. *The New Republic*, January 3.

Richards, D. A. J. (1993). *Conscience and the Constitution: History, Theory, and Law of the Reconstruction Amendments*. Princeton, NJ: Princeton University Press.

Warner, M. (2000). Disruptions. *The Village Voice*, June 21.

from the Arab World

GENDER VIOLENCE

———

Raja Ben Slama

Translated by Robert Bononno

IT IS TOLD THAT one of the Umayyad caliphs ordered the governor of Medina to register every "effeminate" singer in the holy city. However, in Arabic, a single diacritical point separates the verb "register" (*ahsi*) from the verb "castrate" (*akhsi*). So, accidentally, the governor caused a significant number of singers, including a certain Dalal, to be castrated (Isfahani 1992). Considered to be "beautiful, courtly, and eloquent," "Dalal the effeminate" was one of the most famous musicians in Medina in the seventh century. "Effeminate" is only an approximate translation of the Arabic *mukhannath*, which should not be confused with *khuntha*—hermaphrodite—although both words are derived from the same root (kh-n-th), whose most general meaning is to twist, squirm, or bend. A *mukhannath* is generally a "passive" homosexual. But Dalal was both active and passive. Because he enjoyed "that which was pleasing to men and to women," he was what we would now call "bisexual."

Far from being merely "a humorous anecdote, created to reveal the difficulties of Arabic writing" (*Encyclopédie de l'Islam*, vol. 3, p. 8), this story of castration bears witness to the dissuasive violence that could be used to address, or try to address, gender problems and manage the often confused paradigms of normality and abnormality. Moreover, the governor's error is not without significance; registering and castrating are part of the same political act of identification, which separates, assigns roles and fixed identities, distinguishes through the use of marks, and censors. There is no doubt that Dalal disturbed the moral order by indulging in song, wine, and adultery, practices considered reprehensible in the eyes of the censors in the holy city. But what was most threatening, in more ways than one—and what threatened him in turn—was the way he upset the order of normative evidence and statutory hierarchies that support every formally bipolar and strongly andro-heterocentric society. Dalal was a freeman (*mawla*), who was allowed to visit single women, serving as their procurer and lover, and was open about his bisexuality. This is the most likely reason for the arbitrary nature of his punishment, which, legally speaking, does not correspond to any precise legal statute but blindly responds to the logic of the politics of gender: that men who are neither men nor women should be emasculated, and that all those who are unworthy of their gender identity and status as freemen should be excluded from the male order, along with those who take it upon themselves to cross the barrier separating free men and free women, whom the Koran designates by the term *hija'b*—veil.

HOLES IN THE SEXUAL ORDER

God, says the Koran, created man (*insa:n*) but he also created "the male and the female" separately (verses 49:13, 53:45, 75:39, and 92:3). The divine order of gender is strictly binary; there is no place for a third gender. Writing about one of these verses, a commentator remarked that God has "limited the progeniture (Adam and Eve) to two genders only; it follows that the hermaphrodite does not constitute a gender for its truth attaches it to both genders: that of humanity (a'damiyya, relative to Adam); consequently, it is associated with one of the two genders (masculine or feminine) . . . according to the organs that are lacking or in excess" (Qurtubi 1985, vol. 3, p. 1315). But this negation of the third gender was constantly contradicted or tested by experience. In the Koran itself there is a reference to two categories of persons, each in its own way capable of upsetting the duality ordained by God. The eunuch, a "desexualized" being created essentially for use in the harem, is the first. It is believed that the Koran alludes to this in verse 24:31, where it is said that women are authorized to display their charms to domestic males "who are not overcome by carnal desire." The ephebe is the second: a paradisiacal creature, neither woman nor man, but highly sexual, he is one of the objects of pleasure available to male believers. For, although it strongly condemns male homosexuality (liwa:t), the Koran promises true believers that they will be served in Paradise by immortal ephebes (56:17) who are "like pearls within their shells" (52:24), like "pearls dispersed" (76:19). Even though ultimately these categories consolidate male domination here below as in the beyond, there appears, within the very heart of the sacred Book, a breach in the theological edifice of binary sexuality.

During the first centuries of the Hegira, in writings that have been extensively cited, where dreams, laughter, and blasphemy hold pride of place, from time to time, a secularized social space appears, a plural and equivocal culture, a tradition of a third gender, which modern ideologies of original purity and uniformity have difficulty in concealing. Thus, the story of Dalal, who after his castration is said to have remarked "now my khunth is perfect." This qualifying substantive khunth embodies the ambiguity of the root (kh-n-th), which refers to male homosexuality as well as hermaphroditism. In describing himself this way Dalal therefore would have been expressing his desire of belonging to khunth, to a genderless gender. The mutilation that excludes him from the world of men does not, however, make him a woman, nor does it make him a eunuch, a man without the attributes of virility, for he transforms it into an accomplishment. Without attributing to Dalal a contemporary sense of "queer" awareness, we can say that he reappropriates his body, constructs his life and desire outside the implications of his initial gender identity, as he does outside the boundaries of a political label intended to make him a castrato.

As with Dalal, entire social categories have punched holes in the bipolar order. The reality of intersexuality imposed itself on the doctors of the law, now forced to determine the legal status of hermaphrodites, characterized as "problematic" or "indeterminate" (khuntha; mushkil). They decreed that such persons were not suited for marriage, that they were to inherit half the woman's inheritance and half that of the man (Ibn Juzay, n.d.). The sexual remainder in eunuchs became another source of generic and statutory disorder. Nothing prevented these servants, disposed to watch over the women, from having a highly active erotic life (Jahidh, n.d.). In fact they were highly regarded as lovers because "their erection is rapid and ejaculation slow to occur" and there was no risk of conception. The prologue to the Thousand and One Nights testifies to this. In it the horrified sultan discovers that his wife has been having sexual relations with his black eunuch. In the legal sphere lawyers question eunuchs' ability to lead prayers, but acknowledge that they can take wives.

The Koran does not use the term mukhannath, which is relatively neutral and tinged with humor, to characterize male homo-

sexuality but rather liwa:t, a noun derived from Lu:t, the translation of the Biblical prophet Lot. In several verses (7:79–91,
27:54–55, and 26:165) the Koran denounces this vice and recalls the punishment God inflicted on Lot's people for having
succumbed to it. Referring to verse 4:15, where it is said, "If
any of your women is guilty of unnatural offense, bring four of
your witnesses to give evidence; if they testify against them,
retain them in the houses until death overtakes them or God
provides some other way for them" (Blachère, 1947–1950),
some commentators have given the meaning lesbianism to the
term turpitude (fa:hicha), rather than adultery or fornication. The
conclusion was that lesbians could be legally kept in the home
until death.

It seems, however, that these sexual orientations were widely
tolerated. Just as the prohibition against wine did not prevent
people from drinking or celebrating its virtues in poetry, the
prohibition against homosexuality did not prevent such illicit
love or its glorification. One didn't have to wait to reach Paradise to enjoy the love of the ephebe. Kings such as Aghlabide
Ibrahim II and the Abbasid caliphs like al-Amin and al-Mu'tasim
surrounded themselves with young boys. Ghulamiyyat, young
women dressed as boys, spread fantasies of ambiguity throughout the courts of the caliphs and the salons. Beginning in the
eighth century, there was an aesthetic and erotic turning point
in Arabic culture leading to the celebration of homosexuality and
homosexual love. A poetic genre was now devoted to the love
of young boys. Poets like Abu Nuas elegized immodesty and sang
of wine, adultery, and homosexuality, while enjoying widespread fame among the nobility and the common people. In one
of his poems al-Jahiz (d. 869) describes a debate between a
connoisseur of women and a connoisseur of young boys. The
latter presents the love of women as a sign of "bedouinness,"
that is to say, a sign of rusticity and austerity, whereas the refined

pleasures obtained from boys assumed a high degree of civilization. To the famous legends of courtly heterosexual love were now added stories of homosexual love that were as highly regarded and that provided idealized figures with which readers could identify. The bibliography by Ibn Nadim (d. 1047) contains a number of titles of love stories in which male and female names appear with equal frequency. *The Dove's Necklace*, by the Andalusian ibn-Hazm (994–1064), includes biographies of lovers who, like the poet and grammarian, Ahmed ibn-Kulayb, died of grief for the love of a man—a love that aroused neither contempt nor condemnation. Passive homosexuality does not appear to have inspired the same disgust as it did among the Romans, and words such as "lover" (*'a:shiq*) and "beloved" (*ma'shu:q*), vague terms without specific sexual connotations, were used to refer to two homosexual partners, at least in the biographies of lovers. A variety of paraphilic erotic practices leading to sexual and statutory disorders (for example, situations in which the master is sodomized by male slaves—Tifachi, 1997), found their place in love manuals that include the *Kita:b al-sahha:qat* (*Book of the Lesbians*) by Saymari (ninth century), the *Nuzhat al-alba:b* (*The Delight of Hearts*) by Tifachi (thirteenth century), and the *Al-Raoudh al-'a:tir* (*The Perfumed Garden*) by Nefzaoui (sixteenth century).

The Koran is silent about the punishment for male homosexuality. The first caliphs, it seems, applied horrific forms of capital punishment. Homosexuals were buried beneath rubble, stoned, or thrown from the top of a minaret. The Hanbalites, the most severe of the judges, preferred stoning, most of the others flagellation, with or without banishment, depending on whether the guilty party was single or married (*muhsan*). But since homosexuality did not result in conception or the "mixing of genealogies," the sentences evolved toward a less severe discretionary punishment determined by the judge. For ibn-Hazm, who was also a judge, the number of lashes given to a homosexual could be reduced to ten (*al-Muhalla*). As with the adulterer, the proof of the crime was difficult to determine because the law required the presence of four unimpeachable eyewitnesses, which made sanctions almost impossible to apply. This helps explain the sometimes arbitrary and violent nature of the punishment, as in the story of Dalal: the political authorities decided to reestablish order and to conduct a campaign of moral cleansing that did not necessarily involve the application of precise legal guidelines. However, none of the arbitrary punishments, the sanctions of the various legal schools, the moralism of preachers, or the Hanbalites had any effect on public immorality or the culture of homosexuality and sexual outsiders. Muslims of the first centuries of the Hegira were able to create broad zones of tolerance between the law and desire, benefiting, as the poets relate, from moments when the censors and guardians of the sacred slept. In spite of everything, God is clement and merciful, sin leads to repentance, and repentance is the other side of sin. The authorities were able to emasculate Dalal but not extinguish his sarcasm or his songs.

MODERN FEARS

The sexual morality of modern Arabs has gradually darkened with the adoption of methods of punishment and liability developed by the modern Western state and the breaking waves of the "Islamic awakening." The birth of the strict wahhabite movement in Saudi Arabia in the eighteenth century and the foundation, during the 1920s, of the Egyptian movement, the Muslim Brothers, are the most significant aspects of this "awakening," which is characterized primarily by the rejection of a secularized social space and the fiction of original purity and homogeneity. The prohibitions imposed by a kind of Western modernity, especially with respect to homosexuality, have served to strengthen the prohibitions of Muslim law. The joyous blend of genders among the ancients has given way to sacred horror and anger.

Modern morality has reaffirmed sexual bipolarity, the obfuscation of sexual ambiguities of biological origin (intersexuality), and the rejection of transsexuality. Whereas earlier judges absolved hermaphrodites and tried to grant them a legal status, the moderns generate confusion. The story of Samia is one such example. Samia is a Tunisian intersexual who was given the male name Sami and identified as a man, but who had an operation to resolve his/her sexual ambiguity. The judges, in an order issued by the court of appeals of the city of Tunis on December 22, 1993, rejected Samia's request to change her civil status. Arguing that the applicable law was silent on the question and rejecting French case law, which since 1992 has acknowledged the right to change one's sex, the judge decided to make use of Muslim law, which had never ruled on a case of transsexualism. Sami(a) was treated not as a hermaphrodite, but rather as a homosexual, as a deviant who "has arbitrarily and deliberately modified his sex," transgressing the sacred order, that is, the order of nature instituted by God. The following verse from the Koran (13:8) was cited: "God is cognizant of what every female carries in her womb, or what the wombs want or exceed (of their disburdening time)." A hadith of the prophet was also cited: "God curses men who want to resemble women and women who want to resemble men" (Redissi and Ben Abid 1991).

Today, homosexuality is illegal in many Arab countries, subject to capital punishment in Saudi Arabia, Sudan, Yemen, and

Mauritania, to fourteen years of imprisonment in the United Arab Emirates, to seven years in Libya, and to three years in Morocco. In countries where it is not explicitly forbidden by law, the "sons of Lot" are subject to arrest and harassment. One such example is the arrest of fifty-two Egyptian men in a nightclub on May 11, 2001, who were accused of homosexuality. Charged with "violating the teachings of religion and the propagation of depraved ideas and sexual immorality," they were brought before the National Security Court and twenty-three were condemned to prison terms involving forced labor, ranging from three to five years, without the possibility of appeal. The Cairo press went wild, claiming that the "perverts" were "devil worshipers" who "maintained relationships with Zionist movements, organized gay pilgrimages to Israel, and participated in homosexual orgies" (Kéfi 2001, p. 66). While having recourse to sharia law, they ignored the more clement opinions of the older jurists, and overlooked the condition traditionally required for determining the proof of crime, namely, the presence of four eyewitnesses at the moment of the fulfillment of the sexual act. As with the Samia affair, there is the same willful ignorance of the legal subtleties of the past, an ignorance not compensated for by a new reference to human rights. Faced with the delirium of rejection and demonization, the Egyptian authorities preferred to placate Islamist activists. As for Egyptian human rights organizations, they remained silent or distanced themselves from the accused.

As with neofundamentalist literature, reference was now made to "perverts" and sexual "deviants" (shawa:dh). While the Elders situated homosexuality within the domain of nature and anatomy, referred to animal homosexuality (Jahidh, III:204), considered lesbianism a form of "natural envy," and attributed homosexuality to biological anomalies such as the lack of warmth in men, the atrophy of the uterus (Tifachi 1997) or growth of the clitoris in women (Avicenna, II:1691), the moderns consider homosexuality to be an unnatural vice not even found in animals (Jaziri 1998). Moreover, it is not psychiatric or psychoanalytic pathology that was used to sustain this "de-naturalization" of homosexuality but a form of demonology, together with an imagined identity on the part of the community, whose purification involved the elimination of the Other and those who maintain relations with it. The homosexual was said to traffic with the devil; he is the representative of Western or Israeli aggressors. It is because homosexual anxiety was so great that it was projected onto the Other; it was because this diabolical Other was outside and inside, hated and loved, that an attempt was made to eradicate it by sacrificing it.

Obviously, in a context in which not only homosexuality but all extramarital sexual relations are forbidden, where the freedom to control one's body is not seen as a relevant issue by human rights associations or women's movements, there is little reason to assume that Arab gay and lesbian or lesbian-gay-transsexual-bisexual (LGTB) movements will be formed any time soon. However, Arab "queers" living in exile have begun to form associations like the *Sawasiya* (equals) for the defense of homosexual rights in the Arab-speaking world and networks such as the collective of North African and Arab lesbians known as the *N'DéeSses*. These postfeminist movements have made use of the World Wide Web as an opportunity for multilingual communication and cultural expression, where links have been formed between queers living in the land of Islam and in the land of exile. Within these virtual communities those who have been excluded from the bipolar-heterosexual order are attempting to break free of their confinement and act politically, while reappropriating the language and memory of an Arabic tradition of the unclassifiable.

SEDUCTION-SEDITION (*FITNA*)

In Arabic there is a verb that means "to bury alive" (*wa'ada*).
Women in the Arab-Muslim world were not burned like the
witches of Europe, and the Koran abolished a pre-Islamic practice that consisted in burying infant girls alive at birth. But there
is good reason to believe that, whether real or symbolic, the idea
of burial continues to haunt women, who are suspected, perhaps not of sorcery, but of "seduction-sedition" (*fitna*), signify-
ing that which turns one away from God and renders mankind
impervious to His signs. It is this, moreover, that also conflates
woman with the demon, known as *fatta:n*, and that "causes men
to stray and be deceived through desire."

In the constellation of tales that forms the history of Dalal,
there are two anecdotes that blend the fate of the libertine with
that of women and in which both are subject to repression. It is
told that Dalal was in the habit of visiting two women of the
Umayyad upper class, one of whom was the niece of the governor of Medina, the famous Marwan ibn al-Hakam (d. 685). The
two women, who were said to be "among the most shameless,
climbed upon a horse and rode about in such a way that the
bracelets around their ankles were exposed." The caliph Muawiya
asked the governor to chastise his niece. "This man requested
that the young woman come to him, ordered that a well be dug
along the road she was accustomed to travel, and had it covered
with straw. The young woman fell into the well, which served
as her tomb. Men were sent to find Dalal, but he had fled to
Mecca." The second anecdote concerns Dalal's behavior during
prayer. "The effeminate Dalal was praying by my side in the
mosque. He farted so loudly that all the faithful present heard
him. We lifted our heads at once while he remained bent to the
ground, uttering these words in a loud voice: 'Glory to God by
my head and my rump!' Everyone in the mosque was seduced

and the laughter that broke out interrupted our prayers." Both tales, using the role of seduction, address the management of the sacred and the identity politics of gender. The body emerges in all its strangeness and overflows the social or social-religious scene. This is expressed by Dalal's fart during prayer, his presence as a *mukhannath* among the ranks of the faithful, and the bracelets adorning the ankles of the young horsewomen, who express their femininity as they see fit, exploding the division between a private, enclosed space and a public, open space.

Both anecdotes are characterized by their "seduction-sedition," a term that is curiously attributed in the story of Dalal's fart. Screens are placed between man and God, and around a woman or one who is unclassifiable. But while Dalal's seduction-sedition unleashes laughter, that of the woman unleashes a punitive violence. The woman, a "monster festering with signs" (Ben Slama 1998, p. 61), is therefore the most opaque screen, a screen that forbids and separates, meanings referred to by the term *hija:b*, or veil. This veil-screen is said to be a fabric, a gate, or tomb, which is expressed, in almost these words, in a hadith of the Prophet: "It is better for a woman to have a husband or a grave" (Ibn al-Jawzi 1988, p. 133). The frivolity of women is punished with greater alacrity than the indecency of a homosexual; society is quicker to repress those who disturb the gender order than those who mix the sacred with the profane. More specifically, the line of demarcation that separates men and women is more sharply delineated than that separating gender and the unclassifiable, the sacred and the profane, prayer and laughter. As we have seen, Dalal crossed all these lines, but the dangers arose primarily because he was seen in the company of women whom he could be accused of having debauched. In the repression associated with the politics of gender, some are more oppressed than others, some are more seducers-seditious than others. Dalal survived his punishment and resisted oppression, whereas the fate of the young horsewoman illustrates how the punishment of maw'uda was meted out: her body, her memory, and her speech were entombed. More profoundly, Dalal was subject to the punishment of a governor, whereas the young woman's murderer combined the functions of governor and the uncle who served as father. This man acted as a protector both of the moral order of society and the honor of the tribe.

Is there a lack of political differentiation at work in the oppression and discrimination of women? Is the oppression of women the origin of the legitimation of violence? Was the "order of orders" structured around the reclusion of women? Clearly, the ankles and bracelets of the horsewoman are mirrored in this verse: "Tell the believing women to lower their eyes, guard their private parts, and not display their charms except what is apparent outwardly, and cover their bosoms with their veils and not to show their finery. . . . They [the female believers] should not walk stamping their feet lest they make known what they hide of their ornaments" (Ali 1993, 24:31, Blachère 1947–1950, 2:1009–1010).

I would like to move forward in time to relate an event similar to that of the young horsewoman. On November 6, 1990, a group of forty-seven Saudi women got behind the wheels of their cars to protest the fact that women were not allowed to drive. They crossed the King Abdel Aziz Avenue in Riadh and spurned attempts by the religious police to interfere. The police held them in custody for eleven hours and the women were forced to sign a statement indicating that they would not make such an attempt again under penalty of more severe consequences. Their fathers and husbands were also forced to sign a similar statement. Following the demonstration, the Ministry of the Interior made the ban official, in compliance with a fatwa proclaimed by sheikh Ibn-Baz, the country's supreme religious authority, and by other important oulémas. Here the essential argument is based on the legal technique of banning what is legal because it may lead to what is illegal (*sadd adh-dhara:i*), adultery being, according to the sheikhs, the ultimate result of allowing women to travel freely around the city. The demonstrators, who included university students, journalists, and government employees, were fired. The fatwas and statements denouncing the "sinners who display their charms" increased in number. People who had said nothing when American troops landed in Saudi Arabia suddenly began criticizing these forty-seven women, who were considered a threat against Islam and the social order. From one century to another the means of locomotion has changed but here the situation involved a collective gesture, political and deliberate, the embryo of a feminist movement that Saudi society attempted to abort. The arguments banning women's bodies and travel remained the same. The same verse, 24:31, used to justify the punishment of the horsewoman, would serve, fourteen centuries later, as an argument of "sacred" authority to condemn Saudi women protesters, once again reduced to a bunch of preening females who want to display their charms. What are the original sources of this order of orders that continues to control Arabic men and women? How did the infallibility and transhistoricity of what is currently known as "sharia" come to be established?

THEOPHALLOCENTRISM

In the representations I have just given of the relationship between sex and gender and between genders in my deconstruction of the "phallogocentric," or, more precisely, "theophallocentric," relationships that continue to structure the subject in the Arab-Islamic context, I have tried to avoid overlooking the complexity of the facts, the social dynamic, and the disparities among Arabic countries in terms of male–female relationships. Because our knowledge is always situated in a context, I will specify, negatively, the situations I have rejected. First, we must be cautious about defending the image of the Arab world abroad, a responsibility assigned to the Arab intellectual by governments and their affiliated regional organizations. We must also be cautious about the cultural stereotype that maintains the fiction of an Arab-Islamic nation resistant to democracy, orientalist and orientalizing, which imprisons the reality of Muslim Arab men and women in a series of preconceived molds and dangerous simplifications. These include veiled women blinded by the light of day; rich, polygamous sheikhs; severed hands; stoning; as well as the complacent images of an enchanting Orient, belly dancing, incense, perfumes, the desert. It is equally pointless to idealize the past of Arabic women, the illusion of an authentic Islam that we need only rediscover, an illusion that many reformist and feminist writers continue to maintain. By trying so hard not to offend the sensitivity of the sycophants of the sacred, we end up following in their footsteps, mimicking their idealizing and sacralizing behavior. It is through a cleansing process of loss and mourning, not the nervous defense of identity and the past, that a renewal of thought and life, even of religious experience, can be contemplated.

Like the Jewish and Christian religions, but in its own way, Islam has provided theological support for male and patriarchal domination. The monotheistic procedure consisting in "recovering the divine qualities of the maternal feminine for use by a paternal god" (*Transeuropéennes* 2003, p. 18) is illustrated in the Koran in the verses that compare Allah to the ancient female divinities, who hold an important place in the pre-Islamic pantheon: "He who associates compeers with God indeed wanders far astray. In his place they invoke only females (the pagan deities); and instead of him they invoke Satan the obstinate rebel" (Ali 1993, 4:116–117, Blachère 1947–1950, 2:957).

This degradation of the feminine is reflected in the "transition from maternal evidence to paternal non-evidence" and the elevation of the paternal and, therefore, symbolic function. Yet we find in the Koran a tendency to highlight the biological evidence of the father, which results in increased control of the sexual life of free women and a reinforcement of the links of biological parenthood. The Koran imposes a mandated "retirement" (ʿIdda) for the divorced woman or widow (2:234, 65:1), so that there will be no confusion about paternity. It gives the married man who suspects his wife of adultery the right to make use of the procedure of "disavowal of paternity" (liʿaːn) (24:6). It bans the adoption of children (33:4–5). It reinforces marriage, recognizing the man's status as "baʾl," that is, master and husband at the same time, primarily by forbidding other types of marriage that Arabs had apparently made use of in the past. These include marriages in which the children belonged to the woman's tribe and marriages that clearly ignore biological paternity, cases where "the man orders his wife as soon as her period of menstruation is over to find another man and join with him for a time, promising not to touch her until she becomes pregnant with the other man's child . . . the objective being to improve the progeny" (Lisan: b-dh-ʿ, Mernissi 2001, pp. 63–69).

This subordination of maternity and the feminine is made explicit in the verses that describe the ontological, political, and legal supremacy of man and the "ascendance" or preeminence (fadhl) God gave to men over women (2:228). The ontological supremacy is derived from the binary formulation of the act of divine creation. If God created "the male and the female," we are led to believe that He created the male before the female or the female from the male, since Eve was made from Adam's body according to Biblical and Koranic myth. Man's political and legal supremacy follows from the principle of the authority of men over women (qiwaːma), which had serious consequences in the area of private and public law. This is clearly indicated in the following verse from the *surah* of the women, which I quote in its entirety: "Men are the support of women as God gives some more means than others, and because they spend of their wealth (to provide for them). So women who are virtuous are obedient to God and guard the hidden as God has guarded it. As for women you feel are averse, talk to them suasively; then leave them alone in bed (without molesting them) and go to bed with them (when they are willing). If they open out to you, do not seek an excuse for blaming them. Surely God is sublime and great" (Ali 1993, 6:34).

It is this verse that institutes the requirement of the wife's obedience to her husband and the husband's right to instruct and punish his wife. But it is also in reference to this verse that the early commentators claimed that women, like "problematic" hermaphrodites, slaves, and other excluded categories, did not have the right to exercise functions of authority in public or private (*wila:ya:t*). This denial is consolidated by the institution of the veil, which, at the time of the prophet, signified not only the fabric covering the female body but the division of the social space and the reclusion of free women. The spatiality of the concept of the veil is attested in verse 33:53, which imposes this requirement on the wives of the prophet, as well as in 33:32–33, which orders all women to "remain in their homes" and to show their charms no longer.

This principle of authority that requires that women be obedient to men does not simply entail their exclusion from the political sphere. It also has a homologue in public life: the obligation to obey those in authority (*u:lu:-l'-amr*), instituted by the Koran (4:59) and reinforced by Muslim law, which makes no provision for institutions or mechanisms for limiting power. This requirement of obedience in both mirrored spheres incorporates a structure of undifferentiated function, hostile to the influence

of outsiders and the creation of a system of true political involvement. The circumstances through which the commentators explain the revelation in verse 4:34 illustrates this de-politicizing
structure. This verse has been used to explain a history of private violence in which the prophet is the arbitrator but where
his words are contrasted with divine revelation: "It is said that
this passage was revealed when one of the Ançar (inhabitants of
Medina converted to Islam) had an argument with his wife and
struck her. She went to complain to the prophet, who sponta-
neously decided in favor of the application of compensatory
punishment (qisa's)." It was then that Allah revealed that "men
have authority over women. . . . The prophet called the man back
to him and recited this verse, then said to him, 'I wanted one
thing but Allah has decided differently'" (Tabari 1985, 3:350).
The verse is said to reveal that the husband is master of his wife
and it suspends the punishment indicated by the prophet against
the man. But the verse quickly dismisses not only the chastise-
ment of the aggressor but also the very act of having recourse
to a third party, which could have led to a differentiation of the
functions of husband and master, judge and party—in the story
of the horsewoman, a differentiation of the functions of governor and uncle.

In examining the legal statutes, we find that early Muslim law
(fiqh) is based on a social pyramid at whose pinnacle is man,
followed by woman, the male slave, the female slave, the child,
and the insane (Charfi 1998). The woman is worth approxi-
mately half a man; she inherits half of what a man inherits and
two female witnesses are the equivalent of one male witness. Men
benefit from a system of polygamy and divorce, while women
are sometimes deprived of the right of consent to marriage. There
are even grounds for believing that the slave has a hybrid nature, since the slave "participates in the thing and the person at
the same time" (Encyclopédie de l'Islam 1993) and that the free

woman shares in the qualities of a slave and a free person at the same time. Not only does the same principle of diminishing rights by half apply generally to free women and male slaves, but through the act of marriage, in the dowry the woman receives or that her matrimonial guardian receives from the husband, she is subject to a form of property right (ma:likiyyat ghayr al-mal) that favors the husband. That is why the great theologian and lawyer al-Ghazali (d. 1111) considered that "marriage is a form of slavery in which the woman is a slave and owes complete obedience and subjugation, in which there is no disobedience to God." However, as a free person the wife is not subject to the legal strictures that apply to actual slaves; she cannot be sold, gifted, or loaned out.

MONISM AND BINARISM

The binary formulation of divine creation enabled the ancients to compare Eve to the branch and Adam to the trunk (asl, a word referring to the origin of something), knowing that "the trunk takes precedence over the branch" (Ibn Abi-Dhiaf 1968, p. 68). This branch, woman, was marked by its secondary status and an ontological inconsistency reinforced by two characteristics: the lie and the ruse that the Koran attributes to women (in the surah of Joseph primarily), ornament and artifice, which turn this "being of charms" into a somewhat phantasmagorical creature. It seems that the prophet had cursed "those who wear a wig," "those who tattoo themselves," "those who pluck their eyebrows," "those who file their teeth to perfect them," "thus denaturing the creature of God" (Muslim Sahih). Articulated through the fundamental and foundational duality of metaphysical thought—sensible and intelligible—the traits of lying and ornament double the theophallocentrism of a "phallogocentrism," which in a single motion, as Derrida (1981) has shown in the case of Western thought, represses writing and the feminine, or whatever is understood to be feminine. Intelligible/sensible can be translated as letter/meaning (lafdh/ma'na), since Arabic rhetoricians and critics believed that "the letter is the body and the spirit the meaning" (Ibn Rashiq 1981, 1/124); the letter is the envelope or the ornament that displays meaning in a beautiful expression. It is here that we find a reference to the feminine as being on the order of the sensible and the letter: words are compared to "well-dressed slaves," mention is made of "signs that show their charms" (Jurjani 1989, p. 2), and poets are cautioned against the irrational and the impossible (muha:l), which lie in wait for them if they allow themselves to be charmed by the cult of the letter, or the passion for figures of speech that are considered ornamental. The duality principle of active-masculine/passive receptacle, based on Greek philosophy, is manifest in a comment by Ibn Si:na (Avicenna) on the first substance, which he compares to the "ugly woman," a formless being who flees nothingness and continuously desires form. Therefore, the feminine is everything that impedes the manifestation of truth and threatens its production, everything that is inessential but can threaten the essential: the ornament that hides the reality, the letter that, through writing, hides the supposedly transcendent meaning, the receptacle that risks remaining formless. Once again, we are back to the schema of the threatening veil that must be hidden or limited. From man to God, as from man to truth, the road must of necessity involve the elimination of woman or the feminine.

The myth of sexual difference created by theophallocentrism is a myth of generic difference but of biological nondifference. For God also created Man: "O Men, fear your Lord who created you from a single cell, and from it created its mate, and from the two of them dispersed men and women (male and female) in multitudes" (Ali 1993, 4:1). This reference to a "single cell" is the sign of a biological monism that does not contradict generic binarism. In the Arabic cultural space there exists a unisex model similar to the one discussed by Thomas Laqueur in the West and that dominated all notions about sex and the relationships between men and women until the eighteenth century. Language and some representations of the body have retained traces of this model. "Farj"—a "hollow, the gap between two things"—is the name given to the sexual organ of men and women; a man who is not yet married is known as a "virgin," as is a woman. "Khitan" signifies circumcision as well as the "place of the ablation for the male and the female." A symmetry is attested between the clitoris and the penis, for the uncircumcised male is said to be "clitoridian" ("abdhar," which is derived from "badhr," clitoris). Similarly, the term prepuce, the loose fold of skin removed from the penis, also applies to women. Women enjoy sexual pleasure as do men and their "liquid-semen" was considered a "condition for procreation," for the "infant is not born of the man's sperm alone but of the union of the two partners, that is of their reciprocal liquid, that is the liquid of the male and menstrual blood. . . . In any case, the woman's liquid is a necessary condition of procreation" (Ghazali 1986, 2:58). The medical texts inspired by Galen, who was known to the Arabs, reinforced this biological monism. There were references to the "reversed sex," which, lacking vital heat, was not propelled outward, and al-Razi (Razès, d. 1209) believed that "the genital organs in women are arranged inside the belly and are naturally affected by this emplacement" (Tifachi 1997, p. 230).

Since man's supremacy was self-evident, the tautology was commonplace that consisted in justifying the principle of authority that governed private life by the inability of women to fulfill public functions, while their failure to fulfill such public functions was explained by the same principle of authority. The commentators also made use of quantitative differences that turned women into defective men. Women were "deficient in reason and religion" according to the hadith of the prophet (Bukhari, n.d.). Men are stronger and firmer because they are ruled by vital heat and stiffness, whereas women are weak and soft because they are dominated by cold and damp, according to those who appealed to the scientific knowledge of the time (Qurtubi 1985). To this ancient monism there followed a binarism that may resolve the modern confusion over gender roles. It partially explains the disappearance of the concept of sex, since *farj* now refers only to the sex organ of the female, who assumes the human "want-to-be" by herself. In (neo)fundamentalist writings it is the binary component of divine creation that appears to take precedence over the unique-person version. Thus the *surah* of Night begins: "I call the night to witness when it covers over, and the day when it shines in all its glory, and Him who created the male and female" (Ali 1993, 92:1–2). The temporal duality of day and night is juxtaposed with sexual duality, which is made to appear no less evident. Although he does not refer specifically to this verse, Sha'raoui (1987), one of the most popular contemporary muftis in Egypt and throughout the Arab world, takes the decisive step by comparing this second duality to the first. The analogy enables him to delegitimize women's work outside the home. "God created 'two temporal genders' (*naw'*) and assigned them two different functions, as if he had created two different human genders to assign them two different tasks" (vol. 2, p. 203). The older Aristotelian opposition of active/passive curiously reappears in this same Sha'raoui, who claims to rely on modern biology.

In the sexual act the man plays the active role because he ejaculates spermatozoa that promote pregnancy. In this case he makes a considerable effort and frees a great deal of energy by ejaculating these reproductive cells. In contrast the woman's role is passive, for her secretions during the sexual act are not used for reproduction but serve only to lubricate the man's sex in order to facilitate penetration and remove any obstacles at the moment of ejaculation. . . . From this we see that man's role is positive and woman's role is negative or less positive. [vol. 1, p. 19]

There was a transition from a system of thought that combined biological monism and generic binarism to a binarism that ontologized and "naturalized" the differences between the sexes. But this binarism is not exclusive to fundamentalist or neofundamentalist discourse. Arabic feminist thought has often wavered within a form of sexual differentialism that sometimes contains vague cultural aspirations and consequently has not formulated a true universalist foundation for its egalitarian claims. It was quick to attack Freud, comparing him to Ghazali and showing a preference for the great misogynist theologian (Mernissi 2001, Sa'daoui 1990), simply because, starting with ancient biological monism, he stated that the woman is active during the sexual act and conception. Feminist writing falls into the same trap of ontologizing of the differences between the sexes by evoking "women's specificity" and women's writing. The theory of gender itself can unknowingly produce new "essentializing fetishes" (Derrida 1981, p. 43). Recently, sociologists have begun to talk about politics based on gender and even on the institutionalization of gender.

UNVEILING, REVEILING

A process of historicization and, therefore, of relativization of gender differences and hierarchical relations has been sketched by the Arab modernist movement, along with "renewed access to the pathways of personal reflection" (Ijtihad) and the unveiling of women. At the start of the twentieth century the term *sufur*, meaning "unveiling the face," was a magical word, an emblem symbolizing progress and openness and that was applied not only to women but to society as a whole. There was also a journal named *Sufur*, first published in Egypt in 1915, which helped spread awareness of the project of total emancipation (Ben Slama). The Tunisian Tahir Haddad (d. 1935), as early as 1930, espoused the equality of the sexes by asking that more atten- tion be given to the "ethical intentions of Shari'a" (*maqasid*) than to the terms of Muslim law, which had been wrongly sacralized. "The Koran," Haddad (1985) wrote,

> has expressly ordered in a number of verses that men and women be distinguished. This does not prevent it from acknowledging the principle of social equality between the sexes whenever the conditions are appropriate and the time demands it, since, in its most profound sense, it aims at absolute justice, the spirit of the supreme law, for Islam is the religion that has gradually insti- tuted its strictures on the basis of necessity. [p. 43]

But fundamentalist movements that followed have, since the 1920s, opposed the women's liberation movement, asking women to veil themselves twice: by playing their traditional roles of mothers and wives, and by wearing the veil, which had now become fetishized. Between the removal of the veil and the reveiling of women, a new dogma was propounded stressing the infallibility of sharia law and the unchangeability of its pro- visions, said to be based on the prohibition against reinterpret- ing texts that were felt to be clear and categorical. Since "Islam is valid for all times and all places," the dogma entailed a re- fusal of history, the cult of the terms of Muslim law, and a ma- niacal desire to make the female body invisible and untouchable. These beliefs spread even to the non-Koranic schools and are now orchestrated by the Saudi Wahhabite regime, the University of al-Azhar, the Islamic Congress, the most popular satellite networks, and publishers who distribute, at little expense, a literature in which women are held in contempt and assumed to be culpable. And we must be clear about this: contemporary reveiling is not a simple return to the veil, a simple resurgence of the terms of Muslim law. Ever since the Iranian revolution, it is the contradictory model of the veiled but active woman that has been propagated, the woman who will bear the stigmata of the veil without being a recluse, who will appear in public but whose body is barred, forbidden. Thus, the veil is, like Dalal's castration, an attempted gender marker added to the ideological marker. It reflects the intent to reorganize the difference between the sexes and revivify the prohibition against the female body. It is an attempt to de-eroticize public space, to undermine it, and in the worst way, for it is the shadow of the harem that falls over the polity, with its image of the seductive female, turning the contemporary woman into a very special kind of citizen.

SHARIA AND SCHIZOPHRENIA

The legal status of the slave has disappeared without much notice; the terms of criminal law, which have been clearly codified by the Koran, are no longer applied in the majority of Arab countries. However, the demand for political and civil rights continues to be frustrated by the principle of male authority, as in the tradition of the Prophet who says, "the people who confide their affairs to a woman will never know success" (al-Bokhari, Sahih Al-Ghazali 1986, 2:65). In countries like Kuwait and the Arab Emirates, women are not allowed to serve in political office or vote. But these views also affect the behavior of the electorate in countries where voting rights and the right to hold office are guaranteed, but where the rate of representation of women in government is estimated to be no more than 5 percent. In the area of private law, Arab legislators have placed women under the authority of their father or husband but have not banned polygamy, divorce is generally the right of the husband, children born from a marriage between a woman and a foreigner are not given citizenship, Muslim women cannot marry non-Muslim men, and so on. In spite of the poverty of the current political system, there are disparities among countries. In Tunisia, for example, the Code of Personal Status, introduced in 1957, forbids polygamy, grants women the right to no-questions-asked divorce, and replaces the duty of obeying the husband with the responsibility of mutual compatibility (husn al-mu'a:shara). At the same time, the code stipulates that the "father is the head (ra'i:s) of the family." Abortion rights were recognized in July 1965. In Saudi Arabia, in contrast, the right to appear in public and show one's face, or the right to drive a car can be set forth as minimal political demands. But in general, and beyond any questions of diversity and complexity, a form of legal dualism is found nearly everywhere in the Muslim world. This involves "the use of Islamic sources whenever it involves legislating family matters or personal status and, at the same time, the nearly total abandonment of those sources when it involves codifying civil law, criminal law, and, in general, any other branches of law" (Chehata, Ascha 1997, p. 311). What is today known as sharia is, roughly speaking, Muslim personal law, the ultimate guarantee for maintaining traditional relationships between genders—in other words, the inferiorization of women and control of their activities and their bodies. This ahistoricity is a source of schizophrenia. On the one hand, legal statutes contradict social reality, reflected in an appreciable increase in the number of women active in Arab countries, a greater increase in the proportion of educated women, and the increased politicization of women's movements; on the other, they contradict the majority of Arab constitutions, which tacitly or expressly recognize the equality of men and women. This state of schizophrenia has even extended to the negotiation of international agreements. The fourteen Arab countries that ratified the Convention on the Elimination of all Forms of Discrimination Against Women have, in the name of sharia law or cultural specificity, issued reservations on important sections of this convention. The Cairo Declaration of Human Rights in Islam, published on August 5, 1990, by the Islamic Conference of Foreign Ministers, is nothing more than the elimination of the principal rights and liberties appearing in the Declaration of Human Rights and the promulgation of sharia law. Articles 24 and 25 reiterate that "sharia law is the unique reference for the interpretation or explanation of any article of this document." This policy of two-sided discourse provides a convenient fallback position. Ever since the Cairo Conference on Population and Development (1994), the concept of "equality" has been replaced by that of "equity" to satisfy the demands of influential Arabic countries, which, in the name of sharia, expressed doubts about the universality of the rights of women and had reservations about the principle of equality. Women have not yet been freed from the body of the Umma whose specificity has been used to maintain them in a state of inferiority. Similarly, citing the preservation and purification of the Umma, homosexuals have been hunted and gender identities imposed.

REFERENCES

Ali, A. (1993). *Al-Qur'an, a Contemporary Translation*. Princeton, NJ: Princeton University Press.

Ascha, G. (1997). Femme. In *Dictionnaire de l'Islam, Encyclopaedia Universalis*, pp. 308–312. Paris: Albin Michel.

Benslama, F. (1998). Le voile de l'Islam. *Intersignes* 11–12:59–73.

Benslama, F., and Nancy, J.-L. (2003). Du nom au neutre, les traductions du monothéisme, dialogue entre Fethi Benslama et Jean-Luc Nancy. *Transeuropéennes* 23:11–32.

Blachère, R. (1947–1950). *Le Coran, Traduction Nouvelle*. Paris: Maisonneuve.

Butler, J. (1990). *Gender Trouble*. New York: Routledge.

Chekata, Chific. "La familleen Islam. Problemes d'actualite." *Polygamie: Revue juridigue et politique independance et cooperation*. Paris, Dec. 1973, 664–666.

Chekir, H. (2000). *Le Statut des Femmes Entre les Textes et les Résistances, le Cas de la Tunisie*. Tunis.

Derrida, J. (1981). *Spurs, Nietzsche's Style*, trans. B. Harlow. Chicago: University of Chicago Press.

Encyclopédie de l'Islam. (1993). 2nd ed. French and European Publications.

Kéfi, R. (2001). Etre gay en terre d'Islam, enquête. *Jeune Afrique/L'intelligent* 2133: 11/27 to 12/3/2001.

Laqueur, T. (1992). *La Fabrique du Sexe, Essai sur le Corps et le Sexe en Occident*. Paris: Gallimard.

Redissi, H., and Ben Abid. (1991). L'affaire Samia ou le Drame d'Être Autre, Commentaire d'une Décision de Justice. *Journal International de Bioéthique*, 6(2).

Tabari. (1985). *Commentaire du Coran*, abridged, translated, and annotated by Pierre Godé. Paris: Ed. d'Art, Les Heures Claires.

Tazi, N. (1998). Le désert perpétuel, visages de la virilité au Maghreb. *Intersignes* 11–12:27–58.

Arabic References

Avicenna 1. (n.d.). *Les Règles de la Médecine*, 'Izz-al-Din.

Avicenna 2. (1863). *Épîtres*. Leiden.

Ben Slama, R. Le nouveau combat du Sufur, dévoilement. www.elaph.com.

Bukhari. S. (n.d.). *Sahih* (anthology of folk tales and stories). Cairo.

Charfi, A. (1998). *Islam et Modernité*, Tunis.

———— (1991). Comité de soutien aux femmes d'Arabie. In *Le Pouvoir des Robes-Longues-et-Turbans* (sultat al-'aba:'im). Cologne.

Ghazali. (1986). *Revivification des Sciences de la Religion*. Beirut.

Haddad, T. (1985). *La Femme entre la Shari'a et la Société*, 3rd ed. Tunis.

Ibn Abi-Dhiaf. (1968). Epître sur la femme. *Annales de l'Université Tunisienne* 5:49–112.

Ibn-Hazm. (1352). *Le Paré* (al-Muhalla). Cairo.

Ibn al-Jawzi. (1988). *Dispositions Concernant les Femmes*. Beirut.

Ibn Juzay. (n.d.). *Les Dispositions du Fiqh*. Dar al-Fikr.

Ibn Nadim. (1998). *The Fihrist* (Catalog): A 10th Century A.D. Survey of Islamic Culture, tr. Bayard Dodge. Kazi, Chicago.

Ibn Rashiq. (1981). *Le Pilier de la Belle Poésie et de la Poétique*. Beirut.

Ibn Taymiyya. (n.d.). *Fatwas sur les Femmes*. Cairo.

Isfahani. (1992). *Les Chansons*. Beirut.

Jahidh. (n.d.). 1. *Les Animaux*. Cairo.

———— (1979). 2. *Epîtres*. Cairo.

Jaziri. (1998). *Livre du Droit Musulman Selon les Quatre Rites*. Beirut.

Jurjani. (1989). *Les Preuves de l'Inimitabilité (du Coran)*. Cairo.

Mernissi, F. (2001). *Au-Delà du Voile. Du Sexe Comme Architecture Sociale*, 3rd ed. Casablanca.

Muslim. (s.d.). *Sahih* (anthology of original tales). Cairo.

Qurtubi. (1985). *La Somme des Dispositions du Coran*. Beirut.

Sa'daoui, N. (1990). *Études sur la Femme et l'Homme dans la Société Arabe*. Beirut.

Sha'raoui, M. (1987). *Les Fatwas, Tout qui Concerne la Vie, le Présent et l'Avenir du Musulman*. Beirut.

Tifachi. (1997). *Agrément des Esprits ou ce qui ne se Trouve dans Nul Livre*. Tunis.

from China

XINGBIE OR GENDER

_____

Li Xiao-Jian

Translated by Wang Bin

WHETHER TO FOCUS ON the word itself or highlight the problematic it brings about, we have to define first and foremost two correlated terms: Xing (性) and Xingbie (性别). Their tentative English versions are "sex" and "gender," respectively. In the Chinese linguistic/cultural context, their definitions do not cause any problems. Everything seems crystal-clear: Xing (sex) is purely bodily and hence primordial, whereas Xingbie (gender), as its lexical structure indicates—Xing + Bie, meaning "difference"—refers to a social identity produced, so to speak, by the bodily Xing. Sex is the basis upon which rests gender.

A person might be born rich or poor, of nobility or commonalty. But one's first identity proclaimed at the very moment of one's coming into the world is no other than the Xingbie. It is already physiological and nature-endowed. Nevertheless, it is this very endowment that starts the arrangement for completely different social roles and lifestyles distributed in accordance with one's Xingbie. This is historically true and will continue to be so. The conclusion drawn from the two aspects of one phenomenon called Xingbie is that gender is the symbiosis of nature and culture. The coexistence of two characteristics within an identical entity is a matter of fact in the context of Chinese culture. But now, this matter of fact is being called into question, which gives rise to a problem when we adopt the term *gender* as a topic for discussion. Whence comes the problem?

The problem arises from the stereotyped understanding of "sex" and the consequent semantic innovation with respect to "gender." This innovation starts and develops within the complicated linguistic/cultural context conventionally called Occidental. In spite of its significance particular to that context, it has spread throughout the world, exerting a wide and profound influence on Oriental countries. However, its claim for universal pertinence faces challenges from different cultural traditions where the notion of gender is otherwise interpreted. This article discusses the problem caused by that semantic innovation in the Chinese linguistic/cultural context, based on personal experience in everyday life as well as in debates. Its empirical nature, it is hoped, might add some local color to the concept and theory.

When talking about sex and gender, we find it impossible to dispense with the concept of *difference*. Some differences result from natural-born characteristics and physiological distinctions; others display a salient social/cultural dimension. Contemporary feminists seem to have emphasized the latter and subsequently contributed to the construction of another dichotomy: the physiology-oriented sex and the society-centered gender. Though both are constituents of the debate, the term *gender* tends to take the limelight.

The differentiation of the social gender from the physiological sex, together with the theoretical awareness of a necessary demarcation between the two, is the major achievement Western feminism has recently reached. This is the so-called revolution as regards the lexical meaning. Gender studies as an academic discipline is one product, among others, of that semantic innovation. But how did this revolution happen in such a way as to considerably affect its significance in the Chinese context? Accepting "gender" as a concept borrowed from the West immediately involves another kind of problem that has to be clarified first.

The interpretation of a phenomenon requires us to place that phenomenon in the context in which it is used. In terms of the concept of gender, in what sense can the Chinese place it in its linguistic/cultural context for an authentic understanding? To what extent can we control the linguistic/cultural context, a context that we cannot transcend and have to depend on for any interpretation of the Otherness, but that will inevitably stand more or less in the way of our entering into the context of the Otherness? In addition to the success or failure of the interaction of the above two contextualizations, I, as an individual woman, have another problem. Female critics of Chinese origin working in the West may not agree with me on many points, and, as a matter of fact, we have had serious debates in the past few years. But male critics in China have their own perspectives on the problem of gender studies. And this is why I wish to stress my personal experience both as a woman and as a critic participating in the debate. To be honest, I felt it was very strange when I was asked a couple of months ago to write an article that was designed to demonstrate the Chinese interpretation of "gender" as a key word or concept. It is not a key word in the Chinese system of discourse, and it is impossible for a woman to present an anti–male-chauvinistic argument that could articulate the general opinion of her still male-centristic fellow countrymen. The demand for a holistic *Chinese* understanding of "gender" arises from a metaphysical desire that has proved to be both phallocentric and Eurocentric. In other words, the demand for the Chinese authenticity in that sense is a double violence. The only thing that can justify the claim to my Chinese characteristics and the right to speak in the name of "we" is the fact that I was born and brought up within the Chinese linguistic community and, as a native speaker, I write in Chinese for the Chinese. To abstract and isolate me either as the woman or as the Chinese is equally misleading, and sounds more European than Chinese.

With those precautionary remarks, we can return to the problem of gender as a newly created concept. The semantic innovation works as a reaction to what is called essentialism manifest in women's studies. It is said that natural/physiological difference results in the social division of labor, that the fatalistic element intrinsic to that difference mystifies this kind of identity with a tinge of tragedy, especially in its application to women, and that this inborn difference anticipates the inexorable doom for women, providing the natural basis for social inequality in terms of the relationship between women and men. This argument is under attack now and labeled by postmodern feminists "essentialistic." One of its most important achievements is to substitute *gender* for *sex* as a guiding concept. By means of such a revolution in lexical meaning, feminists hope to put an end to the traditional idea that "physiological distinctions between women and men constitutes the ever-existing sources of inequality." This semantic innovation might be traced back to *The Second Sex* in which Simone de Beauvoir states, "One is not born, but rather becomes, a woman; . . . it is civilization as a whole that produces this creature." The expressions "become" and "produce" foreground the social factors and push into the background the congenital, biological ones. The idea of women produced in society facilitates an attempt to obscure the relevance of physiological differences to the problem concerned. In other words, the study of identity and inequality in terms of women and men is to be placed exclusively in a context of social hierarchy. Difference caused by nature is diluted or put aside.

When the revolution or the concept of gender imposes itself on us—nobody in China will deny the fact that it is a concept introduced from the West—how can we deal with it through the interaction of the two contextualizations I have mentioned?

In the past, when the power of nature prevailed over everything, people had to subject their behavior to the dictates of physiological differences upon which they established a series of ethic norms with a view to keeping the male-centric society in order. Thanks to the difference based on the physiological sex, women stayed in caves/houses and were responsible for human reproduction, while men exposed themselves to the outside hardships, fighting for human existence itself. The division of humanity into two classes of individuals went hand in hand with the division of labor. It boiled down to a stereotype—female/domesticities versus male/careerism—a stereotype applicable to all versions of human civilization and persisting for thousands of years. It constituted the basis of civilization. Then, one day it turned out to be an obstacle to the further development of history and human progress. It has become problematic, only because history is man's history, not merely the process of nature's evolution.

Confronted with an identical destiny, the West differs from the East in its attitude toward nature. In contrast to the Oriental cosmological viewpoint that one should follow the course of nature, the subjugation of nature hallmarks every significant step in the process of civilization in the West. Then, this desire to be the master of natural phenomena seems to have found expression somehow in an attempt to exclude/suppress those bodily, physiological features so as to reduce what constitutes a woman to a simple matter of social/cultural arrangement.

To do justice to that attempt, we allow for its significance to women's liberation both in the East and in the West. Equality and even homogeneity in terms of the social relationship between women and men once became the goal of the political campaign for women's liberation. In China, Mao Ze-dong put forward the famous theory that "men and women are the same." In its application to the Chinese social life, several generations of women have experienced what might be called "learning to be men," gaining and suffering at the same time. It strikes us now that equality in social activities might lead to women's self-effacement at another level, if that equality should be achieved by blurring the biological differences as the basic determiner that distinguishes female from male. Otherwise put, women found, in the social practice for achieving homogeneity in the name of equality, harder demands on our physical lives and a social existence remote from the identity we desire. This is the lesson we have drawn from past experience, and now few Chinese women think that they can afford to subordinate their physical/biological distinctions to the idea of social equality. This perspective is alien to the highly politicized vision of many feminists in the West. What appears strange to us is the sharp contrast between their attitude toward nature in general, and natural surroundings in particular, on the one hand, and, on the other, their stubborn and deliberate suspension and devaluation of the significance of the nature-endowed distinctions that make women women. What is basic has been excluded from their theoretical construction. Of course, this does not mean that I argue for a holistic approach to Western feminism. There are different voices in the

West concerning the pertinence of the biological distinctions to the construction of a critical theory. The shift from women's studies to gender studies has provided a good variety of approaches and opportunities. But the situation becomes more complicated in China. The complication is caused, at least in part, by the reduction of multioriented theories to a master concept— *feminism*, a few years ago, and now *gender*. To a large extent, problems arise from the introduction/translation of gender as an embracing concept and its subsequent discursive hegemony.

To locate the problem, we have to reexamine the context that makes the operation of the term *gender* possible. Gender, first and foremost, stands for a grammatical category and therefore proves to be a matter of cultural arbitrariness. It implies an action of selecting in society. This extremely important etymological significance contained in its current usage is missing in its Chinese counterpart Xingbie. What is more, even in the West, it was not until the 1970s that the term *gender* amplified its scope from a grammatical category into a key word or master concept in various theories under the rubric of gender studies. Joan W. Scott (1988) states that feminists have so frequently employed the term to reveal the social structure of the relationship between women and men, and the semantic transformation has happened so quickly that the newly created sense of the word *gender* could not be located in any explanations offered by dictionaries and encyclopedias of social sciences. It could amount to a neologism, invented allegedly by American feminists as a reaction to biological determinism. The invention differentiates sex from gender: the former now refers only to physiological features including sexual desire, constituting our inborn properties, whereas the latter is explained as the social constituents, belonging to the category of norms acquired in society. It seems to be a reformulation of Simone de Beauvoir's assertion that "one is not born, but rather becomes, a woman." Now it appears that *female* concerns sex while *woman* as a social being is something acquired and should be discussed with reference to gender. All this recalls an old pattern, as old as the Western culture: nature versus culture. The semantic innovation symbolizes another step forward in the colonization of nature by culture. This is the context indispensable to the signification of the concept of gender, a context in default of which *gender* as a new term came into China in the 1990s, translated as "social Xingbie." Here starts the problem.

As has been mentioned, gender has no position in the structure of the Chinese language. There is no morphological differentiation in terms of gender, person, tense, and so forth. Ideas are shaped in language, and Chinese, as a system of signs, does not provide a linguistic context in which *gender* in the Western sense could occur. With this in mind, one is not surprised to find that there used to be only one personal pronoun in Chinese standing for two separate concepts in English: 他 (Ta) for both he/him and she/her. In the 1930s, a well-known writer, Liu Banlong, coined a new ideogram word 她 by changing the radical 亻 (meaning "human") into 女 (meaning "female"). But, in speech, both 他 (he) and 她 (she) still share an identical pronunciation *Ta*. That explains why even advanced learners of the English language in China tend to confuse *she* and *he* in English conversations, though they can write perfectly good English. Chinese as a language has shaped a kind of consciousness in which *she* and *he* as concepts are not differentiated from each other. It would be a great surprise to the Chinese to be told that there is such a classification in European prosody as feminine ending and masculine ending, feminine rhyme and masculine rhyme. Who could imagine in China that the famous line, "To be, or not to be; that is the question," is a typical example of the "feminine ending"?

The difficulty in rendering the European notion of gender, in the final analysis, is that there is no such word in Chinese. Even the compound noun Xingbie is a modern coinage! It seems paradoxical that on the one hand cultural discourses provide countless examples for minute descriptions about the socially imposed differences between women and men, and, on the other hand, one cannot find a general concept like gender capable of anchoring their shared semantic features. The Chinese depend on other categories, much wider in scope and more abstract than gender, for the purpose of generalization. They are Yin and Yang. Yin is conventionally explained as a type-sign representing Earth, the moon, negative, women, the female, femininity, and so forth, and the opposite is Yang. This well-known explanation is somewhat misleading. For it is perfectly justifiable for Yin to signify the other side of the coin: heaven, the sun, positive, men, the male, masculinity, and so on and let their opposites or correspondents be expressed by Yang. The key point is that Yin and Yang, to the Chinese mind, are not concepts of substance but concepts of function. The relationship between Yin and Yang is reciprocal, interdependent, and mutually determining. So is the case with the relationship of femininity to masculinity or that of biological sex to social gender. This cosmological vision places the women–men relationship in a wider horizon for comprehension. It is beyond the reach of gender either as a grammatical category or as an ideological concept.

Social Xingbie, the current Chinese translation of gender, seems to emphasize the acquiredness of Xingbie by adding an epithet "social." Since Xingbie in Chinese cannot exclude the biological underpinning, one has to modify its meaning to meet the needs of translation. But translation is an explanation not only of the source text but also of the target text. Apart from the technical requirements of translation, social Xingbie reveals again a

deep-rooted problem existing in the modernization of Chinese
intellectual life: in the past one hundred years or more we have
borrowed concepts from the West to reinterpret our cultural heritage and now they have constituted the main body of a conceptual system adopted by social sciences and the humanities in China.
Now, we find another attempt to assimilate local wisdom: reduc-
ing the Chinese Xingbie to gender. Like the old slogan "men and
women are the same" with regard to their social responsibilities,
gender or social Xingbie has become a fashionable term among
Chinese female intellectuals who are susceptible to political/ideo-
logical manipulation. It claims to be the voice of women, not of
the Party; the needs of women, not those of the country. Here is
an attempt at isolating the problem of Xingbie from its wider social
context on the one hand and from its biological basis on the other.

As far as the idea of choosing one's own identity, the underlying principle of gender, is concerned, Xingbie in its original
Chinese sense is a kind of choosing, selecting, differentiating.
Under the category of gender studies, becoming homosexual or
altering one's inborn biological position is a re-selection of one's
identity in society. Under the category of Xingbie, the arrangement of women–men relations within the Yin–Yang framework
is also a cultural/social selection. No one can justify the superi-
ority of gender over Xingbie!

Difference in selection also finds expression in the process of
women's liberation. In China, feminism has never been a theoretical weapon that could be used in women's struggle for their
social/political liberation. Rather, women used to rely on the
ideas of patriotism and socialism, ideas shared by their fellow
countrymen. The choice was made because women and men in
China faced the same problems: feudalistic institutions, foreign
invasion, poverty, war, and so forth. National independence,
democratic revolution, and women's liberation went hand in

hand. The cooperation continues in the process of the country's reconstruction. This is the situation that makes Chinese women different from their Western counterparts.

If gender, a new concept borrowed from the West, does not necessarily imply a homogeneous and conformist interpretation of a social identity in terms of the women–men relationship within the structure of contemporary politics, then what is the perspective one might gain with resort to the Chinese category Xingbie?

In a cultural tradition whose cosmological view demands a syncretism of Heaven and man or natural phenomena and cultural affairs, the notion of Xingbie serves as a converging point where natural orders and social institutions meet. It is by virtue of Xingbie that man demonstrates simultaneously his inborn attributes and cultivated properties, becoming a particular man or woman in society. This is not a political stance like radical feminism, though it does have something to do with politics. Nor can it simply amount to the meanings of sex and/or gender merely because it embraces both. It is a general worldview, the *Weltanschauung*, with special reference to human identity that involves the relationship between women and men. In this perspective, one finds that women and men are born different, which makes human reproduction possible; that the concomitant social roles women and men play respectively contribute to human civilization and social development; and that the human needs including sex, love, marriage, and family are treated in a way that never separates absolutely social from natural or Yin from Yang.

Another aspect of Chinese Xingbie concerns the complicated entanglement of gender with other problems: race, nation, and class. As far as Chinese women are concerned, this is not a matter of theoretical speculation. It is a matter of reality. Chinese women are not first and foremost women as opposed to men but belong, at the same time, to different categories such as nation, country, class, family, and other communities. Gender is so tinged with different colors that it is difficult to focus on a male–female binarism. Thought-provoking is the fact that in modern Chinese history the problem of women's liberation always takes the limelight whenever a big social event occurs that might affect the country's future, the nation's existence, social transformation, or the reconstruction of economic/political institutions. In that sense, women's interests and self-consciousness are linked not so much to men's response as to a wider restructuring project that is equally primordial to men. Gender problems arise only when national independence no longer constitutes a problem and society resumes its economic/political stability. This holds true even in the West. If not for the material progress from the Industrial Revolution to high technology in the twenty-first century, if not for the general acceptance of those ideas concerning equality, freedom, and human rights, feminism would have been empty talk among a small number of female elites. On the other hand, in some countries like Afghanistan, where famine is much more urgent than feminism, gender as a problem is always parasitic on the efforts made jointly by women and men for the nation's survival in the world. To a certain extent, it is the same case with all other developing countries including China. And this needs further explaining.

In spite of the great success in economic reform, the hierarchical structure, with the inner, rural areas at the bottom of poverty, still remains. As a female intellectual from a rich coastal city, I find it extremely difficult to advocate women's rights during my conversation with those peasants whose basic rights as a citizen have yet to be guaranteed. I am committed to a program for pregnant women's health to be implemented in mountain villages. But when confronted with the ragged, poverty-stricken people who are worrying about where their next meal will come from, I feel hesitant about women's rights and pregnancy hygiene: they sound like luxuries. The situation in remote, minority-nationalities–inhabited areas is the most serious. When the voice of the minority is still seeking a hearing, and economic development proves to be a project for future possibilities, how can we locate a gender problem and emphasize women's interests? Even in urban areas it is wrong and ridiculous to place feminism or gender above other social concerns. In developing countries, women's liberation is part of the whole social progress and should not be isolated into a struggle against male domination. In our world, one's social status and vested interests have never been determined by his or her gender. In the past they were more connected to national identity, the class to which one belongs, one's position in the hierarchy of kinship, and so on. Now they have a deep stake in political democracy, economic modernization, and the ongoing globalization. In short, it is just in the process of national liberation, socialist revolution, and economic reconstruction that the voice of women's liberation finds its own register.

Finally, the social factors responsible for inequalities should not be confused with other factors that might contribute to the division and distribution of social roles between the two sexes but not necessarily lead to sexism or sex antagonism. In the Yin–Yang perspective, the reduction of social inequality to male domination or phallocentrism is a priori precluded. On the other hand, social differences that distinguish men from women might disappear in the future, while the biological attributes that make someone a man or woman will remain. To respect this physiological sex is a confirmation of life. Even a desire for changing one's own sex presupposes an inborn biological existence that makes his/her choice as a cultural intervention possible. In the final analysis, we are the children of nature, which is not to be sacrificed to any cultural/social revolutions. Xingbie as an instance of Yin–Yang culture can never be reduced to the Western idea of gender.

REFERENCES

de Beauvoir, S. (1953). *The Second Sex*, trans. H. M. Parshley. New York: Alfred A. Knopf.

Scott, J. W. (1988). *Gender and the Politics of History*. New York: Columbia University Press.

from Europe

GENDER, IN PROFILE

———

Geneviève Fraisse

Translated by Robert Bononno

VIRGINIA WOOLF IS AN inexhaustible guide, a writer who, along with Germaine de Staël, never disappoints. Like Woolf, de Staël wrote essays and novels. Her ideas are reflected in the adventures of one of her heroines, Delphine. Two centuries ago Delphine struggled to free herself of the opinions of those around her and of a normalizing society. She wanted to create an environment in which her own opinions could flourish, those of a woman of independent reason, the public expression of which would be an act of freedom.

Virginia Woolf wrote less than a century ago. In *A Room of One's Own* (1929) the longed-for sense of autonomy is now confronted with uncertainty. Her words, which blend the "red light of emotion" with the "white light of truth" can help explain how the relationship of the sexes remains a matter of controversy, where truth is not always obvious. "When a subject is highly controversial—and any question about sex is that—one cannot hope to tell the truth. One can only show how one came to hold whatever opinion one does hold." We will find only atoms, nuggets, or grains of truth. In terms of the classical tradition of European philosophy, which has never recognized "sex, the difference of the sexes, or gender" as a subject, the problem may not be as bad as it looks. The truth appears to be inaccessible but the attempt to find it goes on all the same.

Today, in the rush to provide answers to questions as soon as they are raised and given the certainty of our opinions, we tend to forget just how long it took before what seventeenth-century French philosopher François Poullain de la Barre (the author, in 1673, of *The Woman as Good as the Man: or The Equality of Both Sexes*) called "la belle question" could be asked, the one that would finally reflect the question of the sexes. Sometimes I wish that those authors who are so quick to respond to the question knew just how much they were simply repeating earlier opinions.

Because our journey will be long, we will take with us a *vademecum*, an essential item of travel. This *vade-mecum* is something less than a method, which as its etymology indicates, already implies knowledge of the road we must travel. The *Discourse on Method*, Cartesian or not, assumes we know the goal we wish to reach even if it remains mysterious, God or the world, metaphysics or politics. With the question of the sexes we have not yet reached the point of departure for an inquiry that is both controversial and conflictual. However, there are words, expressions, concepts, and ideas that will be of use during our journey into the unknown.

Our *vade-mecum* consists of two elements: the identification of obstacles and conceptual difficulties (within a range somewhere between opinion and concept), and the assembling of essential tools (conventional concepts or new concepts). It will also flesh out the notion of controversy. The controversy of the sexes bears within itself an ontological debate (sexual beings, in whom sex is a substantive, and qualities, where masculine and feminine produce adjectives) and a political dispute (the aporia of identity and difference, equality and liberty as distinct operators). It will be seen that the intersection of the ontological and the political is far removed from any anthropological concerns with defining an order of the sexes, for this requires that we conceptualize the difference of the sexes as an empty category, initially undefined. This is why history is so important for a concept such as this, which falls outside the European academic tradition. For this reason recognition of the historicity of the various connections between the sexes, real and imaginary, is essential.

The examples given below could have been literary, historical, or philosophical. Let's assume that to begin our voyage I have taken as my *vade-mecum* the *Grand livre du monde*. Diderot (1772) divided the sexes this way: "While we read books, they [women] read the great book of the world." We can assume that on the basis of Diderot's customary irony we are authorized to read more into his statement than meets the eye and use his comparison to dissolve the opposition.

OBSTACLES

The Equivalence of Knowledge and Opinion

In Europe whenever a woman researcher in sex and gender finds herself opposite a specialist in another field during a seminar, radio program, or roundtable discussion, the encounter rarely results in an intersection of knowledge and opinion, of the knowledge of the intellectual and individual judgment. Rather, it produces a system of equivalence between what purport to be adverse opinions, and the construction of understanding is based on nothing more than self-declared knowledge. It is a painful experience, well known to scholars, and it needs to be emphasized: When it is a question of the sexes, knowledge is not proof, for it is apparently transparent. Opinion, which no longer requires justification as it did in the time of de Staël, which is no longer understood in its ambitious modesty as in Virginia Woolf, now serves as knowledge.

Of course, one could claim that this is nothing more than the conventional game of knowledge and prejudice, and that the sexes are a source of fantasy, of rationalizations masquerading as prejudice, or denial. Note, however, that there is only one argument that is effective for determining whether knowledge carries more weight than opinion, an argument that involves neither fact, nor experience, nor the accumulation of knowledge, but numbers. Inequality, percentage, statistics, the number of the chosen and the excluded—this is the only means of persuasion, the only proof in a discussion. It is cause for reflection. What role is given to knowledge in the controversy of the sexes? Who wants to know?

Spurious Arguments

The second experience assumes several forms but reveals a simple model of confusion: the debate that restricts thought. Here are three examples of spurious argument.

The first is the argument as screen. The fact that female Muslim students want to wear head scarves has led to intense discussion in France. For a long time this debate was identified with the struggle between lay educators—eager to prevent students from covering their head in class—and religion, an old struggle in France that has been reactivated by Islam. It has taken several years for the issue of discrimination against girls to be framed as the primal element of this dispute, as important as the defense of lay education. The latter appeared to be a political fight, whereas the struggle for equality between the sexes was considered a social issue and, therefore, secondary. This hierarchy has, until recently, allowed commentators to sidestep the question of the equality of the sexes.

Second, some arguments introduce a kind of ultimate contradiction. For more than two hundred years, it has been said that feminism would destroy love and desire between the sexes, that feminism and sexuality were antagonistic. The press, in general, takes great pleasure in lampooning the puritanism of feminists. Of greater interest, and certainly more realistic, would be a discussion of the dialectic between love and justice, the violence of sex and the equality of the sexes. The fact that the current debate in France over legislating sexual violence resembles the one about the destruction of love resulting from friendship among citizens following the French Revolution should provide food for thought.

Finally, there is the repetitive argument on the equality and/or difference of the sexes, on the primacy of the affirmation of male–female equality and the importance of sexual difference. This question is addressed below. For the moment we can say that the apparent urgency in taking sides is surprising. The comparison of a political term, *equality*, with an ontological term, *difference*, is absurd. Moreover, the argument denouncing identity politics or feminist sectarianism, while emphasizing difference, becomes incomprehensible when you consider that women have preferred to remain inside the "house of the universal." In place of the "identity politics" used to characterize all racial or national "minorities" into which the nonminority of women is incorporated, I propose the use of the expression "identity deployment."

Platitudes

The idea of a platitude is, in general, based on a naturalist argument. But this is misleading. For there is always the possibility of criticizing the naturalist platitude that arises in the context of an experience, an argument, a conversation in a restaurant, about the nature of women and men. The classical age excelled—and I return to this later—in detailing the qualities of one or the other sex. Today, as in France during the debate on male–female parity in politics that was voted on in June 2000, we continue to maintain this comparative tradition about the essence of the sexes. The arguments decrying the simplemindedness, normativity, and pernicious ideology underlying these distinctions are salutary but facile.

It is more complicated to determine how this naturalist argument shifts and how it is inherent in the question of the sexes. There are many examples of this, including the belief in the natural flow of progress regarding the equality of the sexes ("It is pointless to introduce laws to manufacture equality since it is a natural byproduct of the evolution of our way of life") and the certainty that the equality of the sexes is something obvious and that, as a result, it is not only possible but within our grasp ("So what are women worried about? Their aggressiveness serves no purpose"). We are led to conclude that nature is invoked in matters of politics, when it was thought that the reference was reserved for other uses, such as the evocation of love or psyche. This is a paradox worth dwelling on. It is as if, even in politics, nature were more important than historical analysis, as if the sexes, whenever they are discussed, had more to do with nature than with history. As if, when it comes to the sexes, history were always retranslated, retranscribed in nature. The use of nature is not, therefore, an argument we can simply dismiss. It is inherent in the production of history and appears in unexpected forms, primarily politics.

TOOLS AND CONCEPTS

New Concepts

In Europe, over the last thirty years, three concepts have been introduced, each of which implies the possibility of intelligibility as well as of political action. These are, in their order of appearance in France, the *social relations of the sexes*, *gender*, and *parity*. They have been used to provide intellectual tools and an image of a field of understanding. Their first function was to indicate that the sexes as a subject are so rarely considered that there are no words or concepts to analyze them accurately. The problem then becomes one of comprehending the philosophical weight of every new conceptual instrument.

The phrase *social relations of the sexes* is imported from Marxist language, similar to the "social relations of production," which treats human relations as a function of the production of goods and merchandise. By applying this schema to the relations between the sexes, feminist thought of the 1970s claimed to analyze the importance of those relations in the context of social construction. For it was obvious that the sexes were missing from general analyses of domination and exploitation. Impregnated with a Marxist representation of the world, the concept generates a reading in which the "social" has a predetermined place. This "already given" results in philosophical preconceptions that are not without consequences.

Gender, a more obvious example, is a philosophical term as much as it is an innovative tool for conceptualizing the question. Strictly speaking, it is an invention. First appearing in this sense in the United States in the 1960s, the concept had the advantage of being stripped of any interpretative supplement, while at the same time being a genuine philosophical statement. Without going into details about the analyses that sprang up on both sides of the Atlantic, the argument can be summarized as follows: The use of *gender* is a way of starting from a clean slate, linguistically speaking (eliminating words such as *sex*, *sexual difference*, and *the difference between the sexes*). This appears to have been confirmed by the now international use of the English word *gender* unchanged in other languages.

This methodological proposition is often layered onto a well-known intellectual schema that contrasts sex and gender, nature and culture, biology and society, material and cultural. Unfortunately, this schema embodies a binary vision of the world, too rigid in my eyes, since I have chosen to use history and historicity to conceptualize the sexes. Using history as the basis of this article discharges the tension inherent in binary representations and the obstacles presented by simple dichotomies. Some authors insist on evading sexuality in reference to gender and emphasize the importance of not asepticizing an issue that is always contentious, in politics as in love. There is also a grammatical force to the word *gender*, and the term can be used in the plural (which reintroduces masculine and feminine), grammar being neither biological nor social but a process of human symbolization. Today, this last use is becoming more common.

Parity, which first appeared in Europe in the 1980s and has been nearly omnipresent in France for the last ten years, comes from monetary and social language. It has been the subject of ideological and philosophical battles, which treat it as a new philosophical principle of emancipation, or, on the contrary, as a political by-product, a gadget. Yet the advantage of the term is obvious; it provides a practical image of the equality of the sexes; it is a "cloak of equality." Strictly speaking, it is an instrument, a good instrument for political action as much as for interpreting the waxing and waning of equality. But we must be cautious in giving it more weight than this, politically or philosophically. Like the sign of inequality, it helps us see what cannot be seen, the absence of women from places of power, politics, economy, and science. It is not a philosophical concept in the sense that it provides nothing more than the concept of equality and in that there is nothing beyond the principle of equality.

Of these three terms, which have provided new ways of thinking about the sexes, I never use the first, reluctantly use the second, and cautiously use the third. For, during my journey, I have
often found older or classical concepts more stimulating than
the new.

Classical Concepts

I'd like to return for a moment to the misleading argument that
pits equality against difference. Here we have two concepts that
pertain to different registers: equality to the political, and difference to the ontological. Yet we know from basic philosophy
that the opposite of difference is identity: we are the same or
different, not equal or different. Identity, like similarity between
beings (but not like self-identity as a definition of the self), is
what is common to everyone, to men and women. Moreover,
we know that, among men and women, similarity is reason,
human cerebral activity, intelligence, and will; education and
citizenship are the rights that follow from this recognition of
similitude. What is dissimilar, however, is apparent in the difference between bodies, or sexes, or sexual organs, and this
dissimilarity engenders hierarchized social realities, in terms of
both sexuality and work. This Cartesian distinction between mind
and body, which allows us to account for the similarity and difference of sexualized human beings, is sometimes quite useful.
For example, we know it is pointless to contest this, that is, to
choose between the absence of difference and an obligatory difference. We are *simultaneously* similar and different.

Faced with two recognized ontological concepts, identity on
the one hand, difference on the other, we can now introduce a
political question: What about equality? I will examine the question in terms of both concepts. In terms of identity it's rather

simple: if men and women are similar, primarily through their identity as rational beings, equality applies. This is the case for education and citizenship. There is no difference between men and women voters (only the time needed to obtain this right has been different). In confronting physical difference, equality becomes more difficult to conceptualize. It is impossible to use equality to condemn sexual violence. Likewise, the rights inherent in maternity are not necessarily justified by equality.

More complicated still is the fact that the argument concerning the physical difference between men and women serves to justify, in a way that is often retrograde, professional inequality. It appears then that the invocation of equality is a necessary, but not sufficient, condition for establishing a rule. If the body is involved in matters of sexuality, sports, or employment, a fourth concept, that of freedom, can be introduced, which can be used to justify the demand of individual rights or the rejection of hierarchies. In light of such physical differences, the right to freedom, the right to act freely in the public and professional space, to preserve one's physical and sexual identity, becomes fundamental.

We began with two concepts, equality and difference. We now have four—identity, difference, equality, and freedom—two ontological concepts and two political concepts. As theoretical reference points they are not subject to the pressure of doctrinaire politics.

A second field of conceptual investigation is that of political science. Two issues are relevant to our discussion: the issue of "power" and the distinction between "public and private." In the case of power we analyze the obstacles that impede women in their attempt to access political power. In the case of the public-private distinction, it is a question of working for the equality of the sexes in the private and public space, in the family and in social life. What concepts can be used to further this

distinction? Which are likely to help in analyzing those plati-
tudes closely associated with the discrimination of women?

When the parity movement first appeared in France, instruments were needed to understand how more than fifty years of
voting rights (1944 to 1999) had not changed women's participation in public life and how it was that women voters were
never elected to political office. Since laws were in place, the
question of access to a right (voting, teaching, professional life)
was not the issue. It was said that women wouldn't have power
in politics. But the word *power* was too vague to explain the situation. What power was involved? The power of the dominant
or the power of the dominated? A new language was needed to
conceptualize these issues.

The distinction between "representation" and "government"
is rich with potential. If women are underrepresented in the
French National Assembly, the same could not be said of their
presence in government in general. Moreover, I was able to
demonstrate this (Fraisse, 1995). The important thing here is
to emphasize how two political concepts, representation and
government, can support an analysis of the absence of women
in power. On the one hand, representation emphasizes the symbolic function of power: making laws, representing a certain
number of citizens, a portion of the nation. On the other hand,
government has to do with appointments made by the head of
state of individuals based on their abilities; the responsibility is
less symbolic than executive. In this sense, because they are precise and differentiated, these concepts are heuristic.

The reasoning process for addressing the public-private distinction is the same. *Representation* is a modern concept of political
power, of democracy, and, especially, of the republic. *Government* is an older word used to refer to the institution of power in
a state. But since antiquity it has also referred to the organization
and attribution of authority in the home. I am not discussing

the relation between intimacy and its resistance to public life. Rather, I want to extend the classic parallel between family and the social sphere. Until the French Revolution, in European societies, *domestic government* referred to the administration of the household and governing the family.

There is a benefit to the fact that the term *government* is used in two senses, one political and one domestic. For there are two foci and two institutions of power: family and polity (Fraisse 2000). It is a heuristic frame in which the analogy between the two spaces is emphasized by their opposition. We cannot refer to the lack of political power for women without also referring to their power, or lack of it, in the home. The two go together. Someone has to decide who will watch the children so we can move freely within the public space. The expression "role sharing" is too weak; before we can share, we must decide. Consequently, the notions of power and domination are varied. The question of government implies the analysis of the differences between those who govern and the governed, where decision, participation, and exclusion are keywords.

The third example involves the use of an old concept to qualify a new situation. When chanting "Our Bodies, Ourselves," the American and European feminists of the 1970s who were struggling for the recognition of contraception and abortion rights were part of the tradition of habeas corpus, which originated in England in the seventeenth century. In both cases the right to dispose of the use of one's body, to own it as an individual, confronted violence or social norms. By invoking habeas corpus, the demand for free choice in the matter of childbearing, which remains a contentious issue, was given conceptual force, both theoretical and political. Through the use of a concept with a longstanding tradition, the history of women is inserted in, better yet, it is recognized as part of general history, our larger history. Although this may appear trivial, it is not. This brief example demonstrates the advantage of using concepts and words that are in a sense traditional; this is at least as important as creating new ones. The classic terms help us conceptualize and legitimate an investigation that continues to remain out of bounds.

WHAT VOYAGE?

Aporia

The increased number of concepts enables us to clearly distinguish different levels of inquiry, one obviously political concerning contemporary democracy, the other probably ontological concerning a search for categories of being. However, in light of the ways in which politics interferes with ontology and in which equality reinforces the similarity of sexual beings, and freedom emphasizes the recognition of physical difference, we see that there is no simple answer for the problem of the difference between the sexes. That there are similarities and dissimilarities between men and women already prevents us from choosing identity at any price or ineluctable difference. Moreover, there is nothing to choose. In philosophy this is referred to as "aporia," a question without an answer, a question that always remains open, "a logical dilemma from which we cannot extricate ourselves," as Aristotle might say.

The question of similarity and difference leads to the same uncertainty we find in politics. There is no hierarchy between the goal of the equality of the sexes and that of the freedom of women. If we can say that individual freedom is a condition of civil, professional, and political equality, conversely, equality conditions the level of freedom required. I can provide the following example. After the fall of the Berlin Wall, women from Eastern European countries had two different reactions: some found there was a deterioration of the status of women, especially in employment and political life; others celebrated their rediscovered freedom of women's being, a newfound femininity, a renewed acceptance of maternity. The first regretted the loss of the formal and real equality of the Communist system, the second intensely experienced the rediscovered pleasure of individual singularity, of freedom. So, just as it is pointless to discriminate between identity and difference, it is impossible to create political priorities between equality and freedom. In both cases we are forced to live with the aporia, and we cannot provide answers or reassurances. There is no alternative, only the addition of multiple references and careful attention to the interplay of multiplicity.

The Empty Category

The expression "difference between the sexes" may lead to confusion. We use the concept *gender* precisely to avoid any presupposition of difference before the question has even been identified. I prefer the German term *Geschlect*, which is understood as both sex and gender. True, it is common to see the English word *gender* used in German, but regardless of usage, the question of definition remains. It is here that the battle between sex and gender has been fought, between biological nature and social construction, or rather, between two social constructions, one material, the other cultural. To make another detour, this time into language: French has access to two terms: "différence des sexes" ("the difference between the sexes") and "différence sexuelle" ("sexual difference"). The second is the more suggestive for its representational richness. Consequently, we could assume the difference between men and women to be substantive. Unfortunately, this does not really advance our argument.

Maybe we must simply revert, once again, to the richness of terminology. When we say "men and women," the terms are endowed with masculine and feminine characteristics. Consequently, beings are referred to in two ways: as beings with distinct sexual features, humans with sexual organs, and as a collection of qualities distributed or appropriated by those beings. Since the end of the nineteenth century and, more specifically, since the introduction of psychoanalysis, masculine/feminine qualities are no longer distributed and superimposed, term by term, between men and women. The physical identification of sexual features does not prejudge the distribution or unique blend of sexual qualities, unlike previous centuries, when medicine and morality worked together to constrain identity.

Therefore, if we no longer predetermine a possible definition of the difference between the sexes, it becomes an empty category, an empty concept. Men and women, masculine and feminine, are four shifting referents. It is because there exists a multiplicity of referents that the category "difference between the sexes" must be kept empty. However, emptiness does not signify neutrality.

Conflict

To illustrate the problem, I will refer to two texts, one by François Poullain de la Barre from the seventeenth century (*The Equality of Both Sexes*) and one by Simone de Beauvoir from the twentieth (*The Second Sex*). The first states that when thinking about the sexes, men are "both judge and party to the lawsuit." The second, which uses this passage from Poullain de la Barre as an epigraph to the first volume, considers the status of a thinking woman and, more generally, of women.

The remarks of both writers raise several problems—that of the impartiality of the observer, which is difficult if not impossible to achieve; that of the objectivity of the results, which are likely to be partisan. Whether one is a man or a woman is a matter of some relevance when thinking about the sexes. This epistemological difficulty is also political. If we must question the status of the one who thinks, if the neutrality of the subject of knowledge is so deeply threatened by two authors who are essential to modern thought, it is because the difficulty is inherent in the subject itself. Poullain de la Barre and de Beauvoir consider the equality and the inequality of the sexes; their considerations are political. Is it possible to consider the sexes while ignoring politics, that is, the conflict between the sexes?

Are anthropology and psychoanalysis exempt from such political concerns? Unlikely. But they do attempt to identify a structure, an order in this conflict. Ever since the nineteenth century they have attempted to conceptualize this relationship, to formulate a structure, an organization. For these recent sciences this was the initial goal of their theoretical voyage, a conceptualization of the invariant, of the way things are between men and women. Presented with this research into the order of things, investigations of disorder, of the rejection of the invariant, along with the idea of another possible order, have continued to deepen within feminism and the sexual revolution (these positions can be treated separately or together).

This opposition—the search for an invariant in the face of what is tentative and inventive—may seem simplistic. The underlying problem is that of history, of the implication of the representation of the sexes in a historical process. When there is conflict, there is movement, transformation, change. Can we claim, after more than a century of anthropological and psychoanalytic research, that the existence of a possible invariance has been proven? Nothing is less certain. Obviously, the substance of that research and the discoveries it has led to are not in question, especially since these sciences have embraced a concern for historicity in their analyses of the structure of the relation between the sexes. But we have yet to determine if the goal of the

voyage is to identify an order of things (invariant), if it is possible to produce a sense of disorder within the status quo (subversion, revolution), or whether history itself, as continuity and
change, provides new ways of thinking about the sexes.

Every conflict is a relationship. The relationship of domination
between the sexes, the permanence of male domination, has been
confirmed by history and anthropology. The notion of conflict
has the advantage of focusing attention on the resistance of the
dominated, in this case, women. Better yet, recognition of the
conflict brings to mind a shared image of strengths and weak-
nesses, implies the tension and dialectic of power between domi-
nator and dominated. Here, I want to make one final remark to
underline a problem that has been generally overlooked. Although
historical considerations of male domination and analyses of strategies for resisting that domination exist, there are very few works
that attempt to address both at the same time. One example can
be found in the work of Pierre Bourdieu. Bourdieu's *Masculine Domination* (2001) is unilateral in its approach. Without discussing his
theory of domination, I want to point out the strange way of describing the political conflict between the sexes in the book. Feminism, considered as resistance to domination, is seen as external
to his proof. It is never considered a source of rational argument
but only cited as a substrate for actions likely to provoke historical change. It is a temporal cause that remains outside the field of
consideration. Yet, the history of feminism, as it is trying to write
itself today, has begun to theoretically analyze the mechanisms
of resistance to domination.

Can we imagine a form of research that allies both concerns,
that comprehends both sides in the game of male domination
and feminist subversion? It is actually to an anthropologist,
Françoise Héritier (1995, 2002), that this question can be addressed. As the voyage assumes greater significance, its goal will
not be to identify and supply definitions about the identity or

duality of the sexes. It does not consist in exhuming a hidden or future order. It is movement itself that must be acknowledged, the relationship that makes history and changes history.

LOGIC AND CONTROVERSY

Clearly, it is important to reconstitute the elements of the controversy, which, as we saw, implies an unyielding distance in the production of truth. As Virginia Woolf says, the truth accessible through imagination is made up of atoms, nuggets, and grains. This is better than plain pebbles but nonetheless remains partial and fragmentary, virtual. Therefore, controversy serves as the site of confrontation between understanding and opinion, knowledge and prejudice, as a space in which contrary and opposed opinions are expressed.

I will give two simple examples. In France, during the 1990s, there was an intense debate about the merits of the idea of parity and the need for a law mandating it. The debate was not about the objectives of parity, namely the equal representation of women and men in places of power, beginning with political power. The polemic never discussed the objective, which was the equality of the sexes, but the means to obtain that objective. Are law and constraint the best means to achieve that goal? The issue was tactical; the controversy was all about method.

The second example concerns prostitution, which was discussed throughout Europe, not just in France. In this case the controversy also involved the means, but primarily the end: Can or should prostitution be suppressed? Is it or is it not acceptable in terms of the emancipation of women? Is the goal to legitimate women's freedom, in this case the freedom to sell themselves, or, on the contrary, to eliminate the sexual violence of male domination? This time the controversy involved the principle and the ideal.

Whereas in the first example there was agreement about the principle of equality, in the second the difficulty stems from the fact that the definition of freedom is not univocal. However, both examples share the ability to generate controversy from the principles of democracy, equality, and freedom.

Controversy is the current figure of the debate. It succeeds the earlier figures, characteristic of contemporary history, of *quarrel* and *trial*. These three figures represent various moments in the establishment of the principle of the equality of the sexes beginning with the start of the seventeenth century. The quarrel precedes considerations of equality in that it is the confrontation of arguments based on value: Which is the better sex? Which sex has a given quality to a greater extent? The claim of possible equality did not end this type of quarrel (which has in fact reappeared during the debate on parity with respect to the assumed qualities of the female politician) but the figure became of secondary importance.

The requirement of equality finds a certain reality with the establishment of democracy, especially the French Revolution. The principle of equality was embodied in law, in legal procedure. I refer to this new figure as trial because the denunciation of inequality and the demand for equality require laws on the one hand and arguments, or advocacy, on the other (Fraisse 1989, 1995). The entire history of Western feminism for the past two centuries is representative of this desire to put male domination on trial and formulate the rights of women. That this trial might be impossible, as John Stuart Mill stated, is what I suggested above in terms of conflict. This in no way minimizes the judicial victories obtained over male domination during the past two hundred years.

Controversy, then, is the figure that subsumes quarrel and trial, and is their rhetorical synthesis. It implies not only the oratorical contest of adversaries but also the infinitude of the conflict between the sexes and the uncertainty of access to the truth.

Although controversy has the upper hand today, quarrel and trial continue to be active forms of the relation.

Contradictions

It is not hard to imagine the history of these three figures—quarrel, trial, controversy—their succession and interaction over time. Although they are part of rhetorical and argumentative language, they serve as historical and political reference points. Each of them refers to strategies of action, implementations of the principle of equality. If this principle assumes a central position in considerations of the sexes as in the reality of sexual relationships, if it has the status of an operator—something used to conduct mental operations and with which the relation between the sexes is represented—then contradictions will follow.

In the philosophical tradition of every culture, the one is contrasted with the many or divided in two. Multiplicity and duality are logical images, which appear today in various guises. With democracy, obviously, the universality of political principles has difficulty in treating sexual duality coherently. How, for example, can the concrete universal be conceptualized as a nonexclusive neutral universal? This dilemma is especially acute in France, a country that has claimed to be the home of the rights of man since 1789. That those rights of man might also be those of women expressed in the words "rights of the person" or "human rights" has yet to be established, either in reality or in the French language. Usage in the other major European languages is more neutral (*diritti umani*, *derechos humanos*, human rights, *direitos humanos*, and so on).

In contemporary Europe, women are most often seen as the particular as opposed to the general. The duality of the difference of the sexes is not representable; it is transformed into a particular, reduced to a part of the whole. Unity is always better, of course, whether it assumes the form of the masculine neutral (for example, the historical equivalence between universal suffrage and male suffrage) or, in contrast, the part that becomes the image of the whole (sex, or the female sex, rather than the sexes, which are always dual). There is no way to conceptualize duality when abstracting unity. It is easier to think of abstract man and run the risk of excluding women or to think in terms of duality and run the risk of establishing a questionable partition when seen through the eyes of the universal.

It has often been said that women were not a category of the universal since they are half of the human species. However, they are also treated as such. In international texts, declarations, or conventions, they are sometimes represented as half the human species, sometimes in a list of categories (race, religion).

What can be done, then, to produce equality in the social and political spheres? Should the emphasis be on neutrality, ignoring the professional destinies affected by sexual classification (part-time work, for example, primarily involves women), at the risk of sidestepping the real problems of underemployment and female poverty? Or should the emphasis be on sex, as with maternity, at the risk of stigmatizing individual development? Parity contested political neutrality as an opportunity for lying. Although neutral, social policies can be discriminatory; if sex is emphasized, they can be stigmatizing. The European solution involving the mainstreaming of women's issues, where this involves integrating a female dimension in all fields, does not eliminate the need for a specific approach, a special agenda. Yet another contradiction.

Whole or part, general and particular, neutral and dual, same and other—all produce figures of a referent as well as a relative term. Deconstructionists such as Jacques Derrida have questioned the validity of this referent. But at the same time politics understands the importance of the universal neutral for inspiring action.

We are not yet ready to leave these contradictions behind. My own research serves as an example of the difficulties we are likely to encounter. When I offer an analysis of the birth of democracy and the exclusion of women, there is a question of the sexual bond, the relation between the sexes with respect to the principle of equality; it turns out that history is sexed, that any general consideration of democracy must take this into account. But this never happens. For scholars the question is particular; it is in no way a structural element of a historical debate. General analysis is asexual.

Conversely, if I attempt to understand the misogyny of Swedish author August Strindberg, for example, if I question the customary psychological analyses (problems with the mother), I discover the advantages of a philosophical reading of the misogyny of a nineteenth-century author. I discover the links between misogyny and the decline of metaphysics, the hatred of women, of the Other, in the face of the death of God at the end of the nineteenth century, of the Great Other. Thus, within the particularity of the problem of misogyny, I can introduce a general debate. But who is going to take the trouble to make sense of a platitude about the relation between the sexes like misogyny?

SUBJECT AND OBJECT

The current papacy provides a good yardstick for what is and is not important. Pope John Paul II has two principal objectives with respect to the emancipation of women: confirming the exclusion of women from the priesthood and resisting sexual freedom, especially contraception and abortion. He is fighting on two fronts: the access of women to the power, which is also symbolic, of the religious ministry, a symbol of the equality of the sexes in the Church; and the right to dispose of their own bodies, to be the owner of that body in a sense, a fundamental right of freedom for women.

Therefore, the Church's resistance is expressed at the two extremes of the field of emancipation: in the place of the final struggle for equality, access to institutional power, and in the place of the key right to become a free subject, a woman's control of her fertility. What the Church has stubbornly refused to acknowledge, therefore, is woman's autonomy, the modern struggle through which a woman becomes *autonomos*, the source of her own law. In today's world women have become the subject of a point of view that is political, civil, and sexual. Not that women during the Ancien Régime lacked subjectivity or autonomy. But the exercise of individual right, both civil and political, of economic ability based on a salary, as well as on their choice of sexual status and maternity, is its modern expression. In the age of democracy this is referred to as women's "becoming-subject."

The customary formulation makes use of the opposition between object and subject. The new subject is said to subvert the old, too often in a subaltern position, the toy of multiple masculine strategies. A woman's position as object would therefore qualify that from which she had to escape. How can one stop being an object and become a subject? Nothing is simple. Object of desire, object of exchange, the woman is all of that independently of any political regime. Furthermore, the object does not have the same meaning for desire as it does for commerce. As an object of sexual desire, whether for love or money, the same if some practice denial, it is pointless to insist on the public (but not always private) asymmetry between men and women. As exchange object, between families and societies, anthropologists have shown how the circulation of women serves to structure a social construct. It is understandable, therefore, that feminism has risen up against this situation, which characterizes the position of women in every society and which contradicts the dynamics of the contemporary subject.

It is also conceivable that the affirmation of the subject may lead to the subversion of the role of the object, in other words, of the victory of the new figure of the female subject. Equal sexual rights for men and women, the similarity of their position in the family, conjugal as well as parental, and access to education and well-paying jobs make archaic representations of women unacceptable, as well as eccentric. This is true of sexist ads, where women's self-image is demeaned, instrumentalized in order to sell an object of consumption, a household appliance, an automobile. To be identified with a household appliance reminds us of her subordinate status; to be identified with an automobile reminds us that a woman is a consumer object, even a luxury object.

Not all examples are as simple as these. Feminist protestors in front of the windows of a large department store that thought it was being clever by using live models to introduce its lingerie emphasized that a body in a display window is a body for sale. Others have invoked the subject's freedom to choose to sell itself, since the subject now has exclusive ownership of itself. The problem, in my eyes, was to have used a living being, a woman's body, in a site for an image, a display window of a store. Is it enough then to separate the living being from the image, the real from the imaginary, to resolve the difficulty? It doesn't seem so. The window in Amsterdam where the prostitute is on display is simply a less equivocal image of the subject–object relation: it is that of a subject who decides to become an object of commerce.

I can summarize as follows: control of fertility is an issue between men and women; it involves determining who has ownership of women's bodies—a social organization or the unique female individual. What's more, if the woman presents herself as subject, she can demand to be treated as an object, she affirms her ownership of herself and can decide or accept to sell herself. Finally, a woman, being neither subject nor object, can place herself in the position of an instrument by encouraging the commerce of something other than herself. A subject where the control of reproduction is concerned, owner of her sexuality, a commercial argument, the contemporary woman continues to oscillate between subject and object.

The Site of Exchange

Can woman as object, as object of consumption or object of exchange, be eliminated? This is the question to be asked at the end of our proposed journey. Let's assume the answer will not be easily forthcoming since the truth slips past us, appears briefly in bursts of light, as Virginia Woolf said.

I have already addressed the notion of woman as object of consumption. A woman can decide to be subject and object at the same time. But nothing proves, as the history of prostitution shows, that she controls this situation, either in terms of her subjective destiny or in terms of social circulation, where the object of her commerce, her body, is in play.

This situation reflects a well-known archetype. We can put it in perspective by looking at a recent historical event, which says a great deal about the social context in which this individual choice is effected. Since 1997 there has existed a new European law, a directive on the "reversal of the burden of proof." Traditionally, it was up to the victim to supply proof of aggression or discrimination. This directive proposed that the burden of proof be reversed, that the defendant be required to prove his innocence rather than asking the victim to justify her complaint. This reversal has a number of consequences, for the individual subject engaged in the conflict and for the objectivizing social representations in which the subject is bound. It has been recognized that the institutional forces carry more weight than the subjective position of the individual, victimizer or victim. This directive, which is intended to transform labor law, also marks a profound change in the representations of responsibility between victim and aggressor.

Concerning the second point, the exchange and circulation of women, it is important to recognize the true points of division. In the West, alliances that have been made "on women's backs" are officially in the process of disappearing. It is not that women have ceased to be objects of criminal traffic or a means, a place of exchange, where other affairs than those that concern them directly are settled, as in mass consumption. Simply speaking, women have legal and political means for demanding recognition of their individual and collective dignity.

In the history of thought it is easy to identify how women are used. For example, the debate on "women's souls" during the period of French classicism (Fraisse 1989) served to settle a theological quarrel (that of sixteenth-century Socinianism) that was distinct from the history of the sexes. Unlike the debate concerning the soul of animals, the question of woman's soul was purely rhetorical. Likewise the subtle use of the feminine, exemplified by the philosopher Emmanuel Lévinas, to deconstruct metaphysics, is a practice from which the real woman is absent; the quality of the feminine is used by criticism to serve a twofold purpose: the feminine is there for itself and for something else; it serves as a philosophical argument.

This is the direction we must move in. Woman remains an object, for whenever she is involved, something else may also be involved. The condemnation of the situation of women in Afghanistan illustrates the extreme violence of a political regime; it identifies its principal victims. But women also became an emblem for the whole country; they symbolized the oppression of an entire people. Becoming an emblem, they were also its embodiment. This was clear during the destruction of the

Bamiyan buddhas by the Taliban in March 2001, when the attack on the culture and history of a people became the semantic equivalent of the destruction of women and vice versa. They were a sign, as Claude Lévi-Strauss might have said. Not a value, a sign, in precisely the way a sign is a site for the exchange of meaning.

Should we complain? Should we denounce the manipulation, the way in which women are again being used? Or should we appropriate this manipulation, and make sure it is used to benefit women, make sure they can also benefit from being placed in the forefront?

Let me give an example. A Nigerian woman was condemned to death for adultery. In 2002 the West mobilized to prevent her execution. Some people know that the *sharia* law invoked to condemn her is a means for opposing centralized power in the country; others emphasized that this was a Western cause and, if not questionable, at least narcissistic (Smith 2002). It was beneficial to listen to the analyses and critiques. Women were used in discussions that had little to do with them. And yet, during this fight, the struggle for women around the world came out ahead. We must accept that women are recognized, even when it is obvious they are being used. We must accept the ineluctable conclusion that we must defend their role as subject, even when they are objects, instruments, signs, and the site of exchange.

And this would be the end of our journey. Women would be already subjects; they would continue to remain objects. We would have to work in a state of philosophical vertigo. Women would have a history, which would most likely differ from that of men. That history would need to be constructed, far from any anthropological horizon. There would be no heritage or testament. There would only be this tension between order and disorder, between domination and resistance, the ennui of endless uniformity and the subversion of the new.

REFERENCES

Bourdieu, P. (2001). *Masculine Domination*, trans. R. Nice. Stanford, CA: Stanford University Press.

de Beauvoir, S. (1953). *The Second Sex*, trans. H. M. Parshley. New York: Vintage Books, 1989.

de Staël G. (1802). *Delphine*, trans. A. Goldberger. De Kalb, IL: Northern Illinois University Press, 1995.

Derrida, J. (1990). *Glas*, trans. J. P. Leavey and R. Rand. Lincoln: University of Nebraska Press.

Diderot, D. (1772). Sur les femmes. *Œuvres*. Bibliothèque La Pléiade.

Fraisse, G. (1994). *Reason's Muse: Sexual Difference and the Birth of Democracy (Women in Culture and Society)*, trans. J. M. Todd. Chicago: University of Chicago Press.

——— (1996). *La Différence des Sexes*. Paris: PUF.

——— (2000). *Les Deux Gouvernements: La Famille et la Cité*. Paris: Gallimard, 2001.

——— (2001). *La Controverse des Sexes*. Paris: PUF.

Héritier, F. (1995, 2002). *Masculin-Féminin, la Pensée de la Différence*, vol. 1 and 2. Paris: Odile Jacob.

Lévi-Strauss, C. (1971). *The Elementary Structures of Kinship*. Boston: Beacon Press.

Mill, J. S. (1869). *The Subjection of Women*. Mineola, NY: Dover Publications, 1997.

Poullain de la Barre, F. (1673). *The Woman As Good As the Man: Or, the Equality of Both Sexes (Men Who Wrote About Women)*. Detroit: Wayne State University Press, 1988.

Smith, S. (2002). À Propos du Nigéria, de Safiya et d'Amina. *Le Monde*, August 25.

Woolf, V. (1929). *A Room of One's Own*. New York: Oxford University Press, 1998.

from India

GENDER IN INDIA

———

Seemanthini Niranjana

It was a dark night and a woman was searching desperately for something in the street. A passerby asked her if she had lost something. She answered, "Yes. I've lost my keys. I've been looking for them all evening."

"Where did you lose them?"

"I don't know. Maybe inside the house."

"Then why are you looking for them here?"

"Because it's dark in there. I don't have oil in my lamps. I can see much better here under the streetlights." [Ramanujan, 1993, p. xiv]

THIS PARABLE FROM SOUTH India, like most enigmatic folk tales, is open to multiple readings and renderings, bearing varying degrees of cultural resonance. One could read it literally, guided by the clear light of reason and marvel at the woman's stupidity, or conversely, applaud her astuteness in searching where the light is. But several teasing questions remain: Keys to what? Why or how does one look for something? What could oil in the lamps be a metaphor for? What are the oppositions of darkness and light, inside and outside, really suggestive of? How does one see well? And so on. The meaning(s) of the parable in itself is not my concern here; rather, my use of it is largely metaphorical, suggesting parallels with the ways in which we engage with the concept of gender. Many of our explications of gender appear to go along with interpretive trends that are seemingly universally valid, rather than look "inside" (this itself is, admittedly, a fraught and relative space, raising the question of boundaries and intersections) and fashion "keys" to a more contextually situated understanding. This, of course, raises a number of questions about whether and how to be rendering concepts meaningfully across cultures, questions that do not lend themselves to an easy resolution. To suggest thus is neither to raise the ghost of universalism versus particularism nor to celebrate relativist readings. What it does do, however, is to heighten our awareness of the varied loads of meaning that the gender concept carries across different contexts and time periods. The challenge would lie in addressing a common core sediment of meaning that the gender concept carries, while engaging with how different cultures work in, through, and off gendered realities. It is the need for such an enterprise that this essay and this volume emphasize.

To think about gender as a keyword is, in some sense, to reflect on contemporary discursive formations and on the issues and concerns that gain prominence from one period to another. Though gender has always been a part of societal realities everywhere, its emergence as a concept and a discursive tool is a recent, modern phenomenon. Tracing the imprints of this defining moment is indeed an important task and brings to mind the well-known keywords project initiated by Raymond Williams in the 1970s. Williams's (1976) project constituted a kind of history of ideas, or more precisely a historical-materialist inquiry into the formation of certain vocabularies surrounding culture and society and the interpretive accretions they gained over time. Analyzing gender as a keyword today involves this, and more, for it is not only about meanings, but also about contexts that enable or disable meanings.

It is often assumed that gender is a self-evident category and that its field of reference is transparent and uncomplicated. But this perception of gender as a stable category—often reinforced in daily discourse—is rather illusory. Far from bearing a static meaning, the gender concept has aligned itself with a range of idea clusters from time to time, making it impossible to explain it by tracking its etymological roots alone. While such alignments, on the one hand, extend its so-called original or grammatical meaning, on the other hand, they make for reroutings of meanings that stretch the very matrix on which the gender concept is based. In addition, the gender concept has been invoked by a number of specialized disciplinary vocabularies (such as, for instance, those of literary studies, anthropology, and history), each of which retrieves and refigures the concept differently. Across these varied usages, and at the heart of the gender concept has been the issue of sexual difference and its manifestations and consequences. As we shall see shortly, the sex–gender debate was about how to understand differences—both between men and women, and among women themselves—suggesting that both biological and sociohistorical factors combine in these definitions. More crucially, it is the conjoining of difference with domination/disadvantage that complicates the question, the expressions of these being culturally embedded. All of the above make for difficulties in defining gender. My brief, however, is not so much to venture a definition, as to map the broad trajectories taken by the gender concept (both in general as well as with specific reference to the Indian context), without going into a full-fledged historical account of its emergence. In the first section, I discuss the major conceptual axes on which the gender concept has been laid out, working through sets of related terms (such as sex/gender), and clusters of ideas (such as inequality and biology/culture). In the second section, I look at how these axes are invoked and reconfigured in India, where notions of gender, equality, body, and agency intersect with caste, community, and religion. In the third section I consider two questions arising from Indian feminism—law and political reservations for women—as illustrations of how the gender concept is deployed under particular circumstances. The last section draws attention to certain recurring problems while rendering gender as a keyword in a multicultural context. Though gender has been routinely housed within the discursive complex of individual rights, identity, and equality, this complex often intersects with a number of other identity positions delineated by caste, community, religion, and so on, that render gender a much more complex category. It is these intersections that will reveal much about a given culture, and the turns taken by the gender concept.

Working off this ground allows us to navigate through the shifting referents of the term across cultures as well. Indeed, despite the elasticity of meaning conveyed by the term *gender*, it also appears to retain a certain core reference to the social organization of power relations between the sexes (Scott 1988). Every culture, as well as every contextual configuration of elements within a culture, draws on this core, yet reconfigures the meaning of gender, gender relations, or gender inequalities differently. To address gender as a keyword in a multicultural setting, then, is to attend to the ways in which the core concept is itself informed by the socioeconomic and political conditions obtaining in specific cultural contexts.

TRACING SOME CONCEPTUAL AXES

Mapping a trajectory for the gender concept is essential today for a number of reasons. It will aid in recognizing the emergence of gender as a powerful revisionary concept in the early stages, enable a mapping of the shifts in meaning and emphasis over time, and facilitate an interrogation of the dominant readings of gender and a reworking of the concept in the light of specific cultural practices and experiences. I shall initially outline the terms of such a mapping by drawing on certain conceptual axes that have defined gender as a substantive field of inquiry.

Gender and Inequality

Across a number of disciplines, the concept of gender emerged as a reaction to the marginality of women in prevailing analytical frameworks, and sought to initiate changes in the substantive content and epistemology of these disciplines. Within the rubric of the social sciences, for instance, it became obvious that analyzing societies in terms of class, race, or caste alone was insufficient because it neglected to take into account relations of asymmetry between men and women. The gender concept was invested initially with the challenge of formulating new categories and ways of understanding that could account for the nature and organization of male–female relations and the ways in which these are imbricated in a larger context of power relations.

As a powerful revisionary concept, gender inspired a number of studies on different aspects of women's lives, but the interface of this with existing explanatory paradigms has remained a contentious issue. Today, though gender has emerged as a major analytical category, it is marked by an interpretive hegemony wherein only certain questions can be raised in certain kinds of ways. The ubiquitous association of gender with inequality is one such rendering, where gender is read as coterminous with asymmetry between the sexes and is explicated in terms of an overarching category of patriarchy. Indeed, with reference to gender specifically, the preoccupation with inequality is evident at many levels. The overwhelming tendency, especially in early feminist writings, to cast the analysis in terms of gender exploitation, for instance, is merely a reflection of its imbrication in a series of dichotomous schemes such as equality/inequality, which set up male dominance and female subordination as opposite poles of relation within a monolithic system of power exercise. There have been two lines, however, along which the analysis has sought to be extended and inflected in later writings, both in the West and elsewhere: the first is to work with a more nuanced understanding of patriarchal relations as neither homogeneous nor unitary in nature, and as varying across time, space, and group location within the same society; and the second is to focus on the agential potentialities of women engaging with patriarchal structures. Both of these recognize the variability of the agents and arenas of power exercise, as well as the fact that these cannot be determined without knowledge of the local fields in which they operate. While this clearly emphasizes that patriarchal relations take historically specific forms, could the diversity in its forms and cultural contexts lead to differences in the way notions of gender are articulated? And what are the implications this can have for the very identity of the gender concept? Some conceptual indicators are provided below, posing questions both to and off more substantive inquiries.

The conjoining of gender with inequality, as suggested earlier, has been one of the most significant moves predefining the field of gender studies. This association of gender with arrangements related to the organization of social inequality favors an analytical framework that could be broadly characterized as stratificational. Such a framework has tended to represent a range of social differences (say, of class or gender) in terms of a common underlying principle of equality, which means that the many layers of difference are all understood as manifestations of inequality. Is it possible to approach the issue of difference outside this framework, and if so, what resources could be drawn upon? Socio-anthropological debates on the nature of Indian society, particularly with reference to the phenomenon of caste (see, e.g., Dumont 1980), have suggested that the hierarchical logic obtaining within caste society represents a way of engaging with social differences that is quite at variance with the egalitarian principles defining the Western social ethos. Working from within a non-Western cultural context pushes one to ask similar questions of gender, particularly as to whether the conjoining of gender with inequality is inevitable. This point may be elaborated briefly. Underlying (Western) conceptions of gender identity and gender inequality is the notion of the individual, which itself is inseparable from an ideology of rights, liberty, and equality. Though this notion has been adopted by the modern Indian state in its Constitution, cultural perceptions of personhood are rather different, since identity is seen much more in terms of a person's location within a group. For instance, it has been pointed out that concepts of person in India do not derive from a core individual with a sovereign, unitary identity, but are revealed as an identity that is other-directed (Marriott 1990). This perception of the self as a fluid entity, where there are no individuals, but "dividual" or divisible selves, places the burden of (self-) definition on interpersonal relations with the other. Such a "dividual" character of persons is symbiotically linked to sociality, the latter referring to the ways in which social relations between persons, indeed, the very nature of social action, are constituted. If, indeed, personhood figures differently in our context where persons are seen as composite beings, composed of many layers of social relations, it is necessary to ask how this difference could inform our conceptual grasp of gender (Niranjana 1994). This brings us to the other main point of the principles on which social relations are ordered in Indian society. The hierarchical principle is clearly in evidence, not just within caste society, but in a number of other social junctures as well. How social relations are ordered within a hierarchical whole, and how domination and disadvantage are expressed within these spaces remain key questions that must be addressed even as we work toward a culturally resonant account of gender. Rather than adopting the equality–inequality framework alone in explaining gender in India, the ways in which notions of hierarchy mesh with the above also have to be explored. Seen against this background, gender could perhaps be more fittingly rendered in relational terms, rather than as a purely oppositional category where one is defined against another (see discussion in Hegde and Niranjana 1994).

Gender, Biology, and Culture

Everyday understandings of gender draw on commonsensical perceptions of the differences between male and female. Gender is not only seen as self-evident and unproblematic in this sense, but also as something immutable and naturally given. It is precisely this naturalness that versions of feminist theory have sought to contest. What is more, the development of gender as a concept has also been a consequence of the realization of the pitfalls in relying on "woman/women" as an analytical category. Though the large numbers of empirical and descriptive women-centered studies were indeed largely instrumental in instituting "women" as a field for analysis, there were several problems as well. This is true both in the context of Western feminism and in India. For instance, early studies of the status of women in India invariably obscured the cultural and contextual heterogeneity of the category of women, whose attributes and activities have varied in relation to the diverse intersections of caste, class, age, kinship, religion, region, and so on (Chakravarty 1989, Delhi University Forum for Democracy 2001, Menon 1999). Invariably, the social and situated variability of "women" as a category was reduced to "woman" as a biological category. Such a conflation is precisely what a concept like gender allows us to critically dissect. The concept thus emerged in an early distinction posited between sex and gender. The latter, in drawing on aspects of cultural conditioning and experience, was seen as going beyond the category of sex, which referred merely to the sexual or biological differences between male and female.

The shifting constellations of meanings accompanying the gender category have also had close links with the twists and turns taken by feminist movements the world over. By and large, these debates appear to have played themselves out in terms of an antinomy between two themes—the so-called primacy of sexual difference (or biology) versus the influence exerted by a series of largely cultural inflected accounts of gendered subject-formation and experiences. This underlying tension is evident even when we consider discussions surrounding equality and difference in Western feminism (Bock and James 1992), which incidentally were critically responding to the suggestion that biology lay behind the differential capacities of women and men in the social and public domain. Particularly, feminist theory during the 1970s subscribed to the equality position, denying differences between women and men and arguing that women must be equal to men in all respects, while calling an end to inequality based on biological difference. By the 1980s, however, certain trends within this body of theory veered around to an essentialist position, affirming and celebrating women's bodies and creative capacities, arguing that these be given equal social recognition (Rhode 1990). Though the above positions differed in terms of their stance toward sexual difference, the equality principle appears to underlie both of them. In recent years, the perception of difference in terms of equality and inequality has itself been increasingly queried from a number of angles, with some indicating the need to distinguish between difference as a biological fact and equality as a sociopolitical one. The attempt has been to alter the terms on which difference has been conceptualized, going beyond biological sexual difference and addressing other factors that affect power relations.

Over the decades, then, the ways in which a notion like "difference" is perceived has itself undergone a change. A number of heterogeneous voices from within the women's movement have sought to draw attention to the multiple resonance of difference in women's experiences and lives—differences mediated through nation, religion, race, class, caste, and so on. These voices suggest that biology alone is an insufficient marker of difference and that aspects of cultural context also shape gender experiences in innumerable ways. Read conceptually, it is possible to recognize in these debates the early distinction made between sex and gender (a distinction, incidentally, that inspired a number of studies on the differential construction of gender throughout the 1980s) and a hint of the later shifts in emphases that were to come. The recognition that notions of femaleness and maleness are largely social and psychological products also paved the way for a perception of gender *as a construct*. As Joan Scott (1988) put it:

> Gender becomes a way of denoting "cultural constructions"—the entirely social creation of ideas about appropriate roles for women and men. It is a way of referring to the exclusively social origins of the subjective identities of men and women. Gender

is, in this definition, a social category imposed on a sexed body. [p. 32]

Typically, studies—not just in literary criticism, but also anthropology and history—came to focus on the different ways in which femininity and masculinity are culturally constituted, across diverse sociocultural contexts, posing the question as essentially one of representation. This tension between biological essentialism and cultural constructivism has come to configure most modern debates on gender. I shall have more to say on this in the following section.

RECONFIGURING GENDER: SOME ISSUES

This brief and selective account of the defining parameters of the gender concept raises several unresolved issues that need to be taken further. In particular, I will look at how these defining axes have been invoked and reconfigured in the Indian context. This will yield a focus on two central questions, namely, the question of the body and the question of female agency. Any culturally resonant account of gender needs to integrate these aspects and grow around it.

In spite of the advance gender analysis represents today over the earlier sexual difference argument, the distinction made between sex and gender has given rise to a number of questions, especially regarding the relation between women and their bodies. For instance: Do bodies exist prior to gender? Is one a gender? Does one belong to a gender, or does one become a gender? If the latter, then what is the moment of this becoming? Put more specifically, what does being female signify? Is it a natural fact, derived from the female body? Or is it a cultural expression, something external but acquired? The reluctance to speak of the female body other than in symbolic or representational terms has often led to an overemphasis on femininity as an acquired trait. And, what is more, over time, the problems of persisting with a rigid sex/gender distinction have become apparent. Critics of the distinction (for example, Gatens 1992) have argued that the liberative dimension of gender in an earlier phase of scholarship now seems to be constraining analysis, largely due to the perception of gender as attributes inscribed upon a neutral body. To be sure, to delink sexual difference from gender is to suggest, in effect, that femininity is something that is taken on, and that the body is irrelevant to comprehend its manifestations. Taken to their logical extreme, words like *imposing* or *inscribing* assume the body to be a blank slate, as nothing apart from the cultural meanings constituting it. In reality, the body is not quite a receptacle but the very medium through which meanings are produced.

Embodiment

To put this misleading issue in place, it is imperative that we reestablish connections between the two principal axes that define female subjects in specific sociohistorical contexts, namely, femininity (as an acquired attribute) and its grounding in the female body. The discourse of gender will have to break out of the framework of both biological essentialism (gender as an essential trait) and cultural constructivism (gender as culturally constructed). A movement beyond would require not just understanding how gender is defined, structured, and experienced within a culture, but also sensitivity to the variations in the content of gender attributions across and within cultures.

Perhaps one way in which this restoration of both biology and ideology to the constitution of female identities can be achieved is by working with a notion of the body as at once lived and situated, in space, time, and culture. Such a focus on embodiment suggests an active taking-on and inhabiting of gendered spaces and identities. Here, unlike in other approaches, the sexed body is neither a mere symbol nor an inert biological foundation onto which gender ideas are written. Rather, the body becomes the very medium through which femininity is constituted. In the Indian context, a great deal of significant work regarding the construction of female bodies and sexuality continues to take place, addressing in particular the intersections of gender with caste, class, political events, and sociocultural practices (John and Nair 1998, Sangari and Vaid 1989, Sundar Rajan 1993). Although most of these practices elaborate on the intricate and complex moves by which communities construct female bodies, there have also been a few attempts to attend to the lived body in the everyday lives of women (Niranjana 2001, Ram 1992, Thapan 1997). Lending themselves to varied notions of female embodiment, these works are underwritten by a similar imperative of fusing the constructed and lived aspects of gender identities.

In many ways, working with a notion of the body as it is refuses to draw on superficial separations between sex and gender (or even body and mind). By asking how women inherit and live through a female body, one can open up several issues for scrutiny, such as how women inhabit the body, what the sociocultural meanings invested in the female body are, how women's bodies occupy and orient themselves in space, and so on. To work with a notion of the body as it is allows us to explore these questions at length, since it conceptualizes the body not only as a subject, but also, more pertinently, as a situated subject. Such a formulation highlights the interface between the material body and the representational body, and the ways in which women activate these constitutive conditions. This will also enable one to speak of differences, within and across genders, without necessarily falling back on the binarism of the body as either culturally constituted or as prior to cultural inscriptions.

Agency

The issue of embodiment itself can be linked to that of female agency, both of which have become increasingly central to gender-sensitive scholarship in recent years. Though the early theories of patriarchy and female subordination give little room for an active female subject, later theories of gender identity and subject formation have, albeit indirectly, raised the question of agency. Foucaultian and Lacanian analysis, for instance, speak of the subject as formed through constraint and lack, and agency on the part of such subjects is seen either in terms of resistance to dominant norms or read as subversions in daily practice (McNay 2000). Little has been said, however, on the bodily mediations of agency, on how bodily practices and codes of sexuality could operate to circumscribe and inflect female agency in different contexts. Indeed, a characteristic feature of recent work on women's agency has been to annex it to the question of identity, with the latter formulated largely in terms of its symbolic-cultural bases. This articulation is most explicit in discourses that mark the modern period, where one finds references to a range of identities—ethnic, national, cultural, and/or racial. Even in engagements with gender, there is an implicit tendency to highlight the social construction of identities, where the bodily dimensions of identity and agency get pushed, often unwittingly, to the background. As distinct from this, can we envisage a more comprehensive, alternative ground for debating gender and agency? How do we negotiate questions of women's identity and agency when we locate these on the terrain of the bodily subject? These are questions that need to be addressed.

The issue of agency is decidedly central to contemporary feminist debates in India. Nevertheless, agency, by and large, is taken to mean transformative, overtly political action alone. This perception presets the kinds of questions that can be raised by identifying certain kinds of actions of women as agential and others as not. Underlying this is also a specific understanding of the domains of power. The delineation of spaces as both public and private, the positing of "public" as a political domain (the domain of power exercise per se), women's lack of access to this realm and their consequent characterization of powerlessness (confined to a private realm, and hence non-agential) are all aspects of this rendering. The conclusions that this could lead to are problematic for women's agency, especially since it is unable to explain the varied kinds of actions of women. As Kumkum Sangari (1993) has noted, such a view would be not only ahistorical but also distortive in predefining women's agency in specific ways (that is to say, in predetermining what is political, what constitutes action, and so on).

Another way of perceiving and recording women's agency has been to document and examine instances of women's resistance within a larger frame of domination (O'Hanlon 1991, Raheja and Gold 1996). This is not quite the same as the previous tendency, and what is important here is the shift in the manner in which power is conceptualized. Power is not seen as a unitary structure but as tenuous, constantly fractured by contestatory actions of subordinates, through acts that are everyday, local, micro, and even unstructured. Among these would figure women's implicit acts of resistance, unplanned, often nonconfrontational in that they avoid a direct confrontation with authority structures, and yet striking an oppositional chord. Agency would here exhibit a comparatively more individual-centered trait, as against the earlier structural generalization.

In spite of their differences, what seems problematic in both tendencies is that we may be speaking of women-as-group or woman-as-individual, without adequate clarity as to what constitutes the basis of their identities. What these positions offer us is an understanding of women's agency routed either through the individual axis or a material/structural one, while at times providing a marginally culturally inflected understanding. In countering the lopsidedness in perspective, it would be easy to argue in favor of an approach that combines the material and cultural axes. It is precisely this edge that attentiveness to the body can afford. A consideration of how women's bodies are lived and imaged, how they are spoken about and perceived, and the convergence of other narratives on them (such as those of community, honor, morality, nation, etc.), as well as how women respond to these mediations, would allow us to better address the question of women's agency. In other words, an understanding of women's agency and gender will have to contend with how women live (in) their bodies, and how they contend with what cultures make of these bodies.

How do we speak of the body's sexuality and its cultural mediations? How does female embodiment happen? A whole range of influences can be identified here: cultural beliefs and practices regarding the body, ritual prescriptions and proscriptions, and norms of female conduct that orient speech, behavior, and perceptions—all of which coalesce into what can be termed a culture's "matrix of sexualization." Such a matrix specifies certain codes of moral conduct within a community and is often responsible for the active espousal of conceptions of feminine and masculine. It could involve ideas of shame and honor, the legitimation of fertility through marriage, a delineation of appropriate spaces for women, codes of/for manliness, and so on. Often, women's perceptions of themselves and their bodily experiences are routed through such a matrix, where the biological substratum is worked upon by the sociomoral order in culturally specific ways. Indeed, gender comes to be implicated within sociocultural practices regulating sexed bodies.

Focusing on the operation of such a matrix in different societies can show a way out of the dead ends in gender analyses, especially since it allows us to infuse the constructivist turn in gender with a materiality deriving from a direct focus on bodies. But where does the female subject stand in such an account? How does she respond to the sociospatial and discursive matrix of sexualization that envelops her? The normative pronouncements embedded in such a matrix are not extraneous elements that come to impinge on a given body, but are constitutive of that very body, marking it as feminine (or masculine). What actually happens, then, in the course of a person's responding to these markers? Are processes so simple and clear cut that we can speak of women as either upholding a hegemonic moral order or as deviating from it and resisting it? To understand the ambiguous and shifting strategies adopted by women in the face of these cultural injunctions one would also have to focus on the ways in which bodily subjects are formed.

Subjecthood and subject-formation are certainly complex questions and much has been said about them. But if we are to conceptualize the process, it would involve, at the very least, two aspects: one, as offering a locus of subjectivity, the space within which the singularity of the individual engaging with societal processes is inscribed; and, two, subjection as involving submission, not necessarily forced, but often, as Etienne Balibar (1994) puts it, "willing obedience, coming from inside" (p. 9). The role of subjects in this disciplining of bodies is exceptionally important, and its significance will emerge when we look not at ideological formations but rather at the practices that mark the daily lives of women. The matrix—of sexualization, as it were—that obtains in different cultural contexts allows us not only to comprehend how femininity and masculinity are lived and experienced, but also to trace the logic of everyday practices within communities. Often these are not consciously articulated rules, but ways of living that are followed almost unthinkingly, being coded in the various practical taxonomies of the body. One of the most significant and hitherto neglected parameters that defines this grounding matrix of sexualization is space and spatiality. It could be argued that femininity/masculinity and the activities of women and men are negotiated within sociospatial parameters that demarcate physical space into, for example, inside and outside, the meanings and traversals of these spaces being often elaborated in symbolic terms. In rural south India, for instance, the terms *inside* and *outside* are not just indicators of physical space, but also acquire different dimensions of meaning depending on the contexts in which they are used (whether ritual, economic, or social). "Becoming outside" or "sitting outside," when applied to a woman, implies that she is menstruating, debarring her from "inner" spaces, such as the hearth. Further, the threshold of the house becomes an important marker, not just of inner and outer spaces, but also of morality. Similarly, delineations of inside and outside also define work opportunities for women. When used in the context of a village, "outside" could mean the area inhabited by the so-called low castes. These sociospatial usages define relations between persons, between different castes, and even between religious groups. Such parameters are deeply embedded within a community's perceptual schemes and orient bodily practices, such as ways of walking, sitting, speaking, and even dressing. It also orders the world into "one's own" and "other," designates acts as proper or improper, and so on. Ideas of morality often get attached to these spaces, for instance, when the inside is seen as a moral realm in relation to the outside. Nevertheless, such a delineation of inner and outer spaces is not fixed, but fluid. In other words, the boundaries of the inside (that is, whether it refers to the household, the caste group, the village, or even the nation) could keep shifting with reference to the outer realms it is being understood in relation to (see Niranjana 2001 for further details). These meanings are context-circumscribed and could be differently configured in other locales, such as urban or even semiurban spaces. What is important is a recognition of the definitive power of this matrix for understanding how gender is figured locally.

A nuanced deployment of the sociospatial matrix of sexualization is definitely useful in understanding women's lives and encompassing societal structures. On the one hand, it demonstrates how certain notions of space and movement are written into definitions of the female body, informing the ways in which women's lives, acts, and speech are structured. On the other, it indicates the manner in which the woman or the female body becomes central to the drawing of boundaries within and between communities. The matrix itself is no monolith impinging uniformly on all women, and there can be a number of variations in practice. Similarly, to focus on such a matrix is definitely not to freeze interaction into a static, synchronic mold. Temporality, in fact, is manifest in the sociospatial definition of everyday experiences and activities, a recognition that could even prompt a fresh focus on the relations between spaces and time itself. Being at once material and cultural, substantive and discursive, the matrix offers a promising way in which to conceptualize gender, agency, and community within society. Whether it is the sexualization of female bodies through bodily and cultural practices, or tracking gender asymmetries in accessing resources and power, the matrix of sexualization opens up a major route for gender analysis. While acknowledging, in broad terms, that gender refers to the social organization of differences between the sexes (Connell 1987, Scott 1988), what is being emphasized here is that space and spatiality is a vital idiom through which gender (and other) differences are articulated and signaled in multicultural contexts.

FURTHER QUESTIONS FOR GENDER

Issues of equality, female agency, and the body have been central to the feminist movement and have influenced the ways in which the gender concept has been explicated. Increasingly over the last decade or more, the term *difference* has begun to occupy center stage. The very idea of a monolithic feminism has come to be contested, and feminist movements the world over are being charged with excluding the histories and struggles of women who do not belong to the dominant group (middle-class white women in the West, and urban-based upper caste/class women in India, for instance). In other words, there is an urgent realization that the way in which we are positioned as women—and how this positioning intersects with a range of other identities and affiliations—matters a great deal to our experience of oppression and what we are prepared to do about it. The meaning of gender itself will therefore have to expand contextually. In India, issues of gender equality and agency in particular have been raised in different ways and under divergent contexts, such that formulating a theory of gender in the contemporary Indian world has not been an easy task. An attempt is made here, however, to highlight some important trends in this connection.

Retrospectively speaking, the Indian feminist movement in the 1970s and 1980s had a clearly marked-out agenda. Attempts were made to highlight asymmetries in gender relations, be it the vulnerability of women workers, sexual harassment, or inequities in women's access to health care, and developmental opportunities. Working with the concept of women's rights, demands were made on the legal system to be more sensitive to gender disparities. In the initial years, the women's movement directed its actions toward the government, concentrating on transforming state policies, be it in the areas of law, health, or employment. The mobilizations around issues of rape, dowry, and amniocentesis compelled the state to take cognizance of women's issues, and also to consult women's groups while formulating policies on a range of questions. Yet rarely did this translate into a gender-sensitive state, for its entire machinery and state-backed processes like development and legal reform continued to be gender-resistant. The relationship between the women's movement and the state has thus been rather ambivalent, marked by a shifting ground of strategies.

What any history of the women's movement in India (Gandhi and Shah 1992, Kumar 1993) will provide is an understanding of the sites of women's mobilization. At one level are expressions of women's agency within the space of civil society; at another level are the struggles for equality within the framework of the democratic state itself, a struggle alongside other groups for better access to resources. The scenario has changed somewhat, for the past decade (the 1990s) has been witness to the rise of several new forces such as fundamentalism, economic liberalization, communalism, and casteism. It has become necessary for Indian feminism to define itself anew in the face of these developments, a task rendered all the more difficult due to the different kinds of identity politics in which religious, caste, and economic groups have been engaging (Tharu and Niranjana 1999). Among the wide range of issues that have surfaced, I will focus briefly on two—women and the legal domain, and the political representation—to see in what ways these debates, coming from within a culturally specific context, could inform our understanding of gender.

Reform and Difference: The Legal Tangle

Legal reform has been a major route through which feminists in India have sought to achieve gender equality. Insofar as the state is closely linked to the legal domain, demands for legal reform have necessarily been directed at the state. In the liberal discourse on equality and rights that has constituted the basis of the women's movement, the state is sometimes cast as a protector of women's rights. Legal reform is aimed at securing and protecting the rights of women (for instance, in property or at the workplace), as well as clamping down on discriminatory practices and preventing crimes against women (for example, sati, rape, and dowry). While all this is true on a theoretical plane, it is also widely recognized today that, despite the granting of formal rights to women, substantive inequalities continue to pervade their daily lives (Kapur and Cossman 1996). This contradiction has provoked a great deal of debate on the role of law in social transformation, especially with reference to gender issues. The bulk of early feminist struggles within the legal domain built on the assumption that law could play a positive and vital role in achieving a gender-just society. Based on the notion of a genderless citizen bearing equal rights in all fields of life, some trends suggested that gender difference should be largely irrelevant to the law. Although this was ideally the case, as a first step it would be necessary to tackle gender discriminatory practices through legal reform. It soon became evident, however, that formal changes in the law did not achieve much; the failure to achieve gender equality was then attributed to lack of interest or faulty implementation of existing legal principles, or, at times, even to a lack of awareness of legal rights on the part of women themselves. The experiences of women's groups in dealing with the law soon revealed that in spite of being an indispensable strategy, law alone was insufficient to engineer transformations, especially in gender-oppressive structures.

Feminist scholarship has also at times taken a demystificatory view of law, characterizing it as a tool of patriarchal oppression. It is argued that the working of the legal system, the conduct and practices of law enforcement, and the gender biases built into courtroom practices and legal interpretations all reflect its patriarchal underpinnings. Others have attempted to capture the contradictory nature of the law itself (Agnes 1992, Mukhopadhyaya 1998), to show how, while granting formal equality to women, legal discourse has itself been constructing women as gendered subjects (as dependent wives or mothers), reiterating ideas of female duty and sexuality and drawing on an entrenched familial ideology. More recently, debates on the proposed uniform civil code for all communities have sharply raised the question of Muslim women's relation to the law. While women's groups have differed in the ways they approach this issue, this debate has frontally raised the question of religious difference. Thus, from an early adherence to the equality principle to studies on how women are constructed as gendered subjects in law, to the more protracted issue of difference, the legal backdrop has seen the enactment of several of the themes that we identified at the outset while tracing the trajectory of the gender concept.

Political Representation for Women

Given the marginalization of women in the Indian polity, the move of reservation of one-third of all seats for women at the various levels of local governance marked a significant turning point. Of course, though reservations as a tool of positive discrimination are not new to India and have rescripted scenarios of caste and identity politics, reservations for women in politics is a comparatively new issue. From being hailed as a silent revolution of the emerging millions to being dubbed as political dummies, women's bid to enter formal political institutions in India has generated much comment, interest, and resistance. The doubts raised range from the argument that fixed reservations would ghettoize women in politics to the fear that women representatives would become mere dummies in the hands of vested interests. Jostling with these doubts is also the expectation that the presence of women will cleanse the political arena of corruption and usher in a different system of governance. The assumption here is that women are intrinsically altruistic, selfless, and caring, and that these noncompetitive values could help them articulate a new political method. Without being circumscribed by these positions, it is possible and necessary to see this juncture—that is, seeing women in relation to political processes—as not only yielding a wider definition of the space of the political, but also raising questions about the ways in which we look at gender and agency.

The provision of quota reservations for various unprivileged groups at different levels of governance is meant to achieve a wider representation of the needs and interests of these groups. However, most discussions of democratic politics have dwelled on the question of reservations per se, rather than examining the axis of representation. It appears that the figure of the political representative and the act of representation need to be understood more deeply than they have been until now, especially when we speak of women's participation in governing bodies. Though it can be argued that the ideal role of the political representative is to convey without distortion the interests of those represented, the actual process is much more complicated. The political representative has a doubly important role to play in contexts (and countries) where severe socioeconomic deprivation has eroded the social identity of the masses, and consequently their ability to articulate felt needs in a coherent fashion. The representative may be required to fashion and shape fragmented identities and local interests by couching them in a general (universal) language. To be more explicit, the representative is not representing a preexisting collective interest; indeed, there may often be no such well-articulated entity. Rather, the representative inserts an inchoate demand into political discourse such that it gets inscribed as an interest, in the process transforming the represented into identifiable political subjects.

Reflecting on the representative–represented relationship becomes all the more relevant given women's marginalization from politics and the recent attempt by the state to create political spaces for them. In contrast to peasants, dalits, or backward classes, women have rarely been considered a well-formed interest group. Part of the problem is that given the dispersal of identities across caste, religion, and other socioeconomic axes, gender has rarely been the sole rallying point for women. Whether political reservations alone would be sufficient to transform them into political actors with clear-cut interests remains a doubtful matter. Under such conditions it is necessary to ask whom the female representative is representing— other women, those of her caste/religion, or the entire community? The woman political representative has a demanding task before her, especially in the first instance, that of having to play a major role in the very formation of women as a collective interest group. In the process, she also comes to institute her own political agency and mediate in the agency of those whom she represents. Hitherto unmarked or assumed as unproblematic in political debate, this relation between the representative and the represented could assist in understanding and conceptualizing the process of women's politicization. Also, while it is true that the issue of women's representation in politics has drawn attention to the empowerment of women within democratic systems, it is also necessary to realize that women's political agency cannot be limited to this alone. In addition to these formally available political roles, we need to work with a wider understanding of women's politicization that can take into account manifestations of women's agency in innumerable arenas within civil society itself. Such an enlarged perception of women and the political arena can benefit from the conceptualization of women as embodied subjects acting within determinate material conditions.

STRADDLING THE SPACE OF MULTICULTURALISM

Harking back to an earlier attempt to explicate keywords (Williams 1976), we noted at the very outset that this was an attempt to trace from within a materialist framework the formation of some central ideas and the accretions in meaning over time. The historical contexts and circumstances shaping the meanings of words like *culture* and *society* find succinct elaboration in Williams. While this is one way of tracing the genealogy of a concept, working through the many uses of a concept can obscure the question of its identity. Our project, in working with and through gender, has tried to inscribe this axis of the concept's identity more thoroughly, while also striving to straddle the space of a contemporary multiculturalism. This has primarily involved working at two levels: one, tracing the axes on which the gender concept has been laid out (as indicated earlier, these have been, primarily, the individual rights, identity, and equality axes) and the idea clusters it has been aligned with; and two, showing how these axes are invoked and reconfigured in India, where understandings of gender, equality, and agency intersect with caste, community, religion, and so on. Implicit in these tracings has also been the conviction that, even within a society/nation/ culture, the fracture lines are such that there can be no one homogeneous cultural rendering of gender relations. This makes the task of addressing gender as a keyword in a multicultural context all the more difficult.

Although some of the referents of the concept of gender can (and ought to) be universally rendered, there are also culturally specific workings of the concept that have to be addressed. What could be the implications of such a nuanced space of articulation both for gender politics and for gender analyses today? The politics and policies of most countries today are increasingly being defined by the demands of distinct cultural groups within them. While the multiculturalism debate has taken different forms in different countries, seen from within a largely liberal discourse, it has meant the challenge of balancing the demands of individual and group rights in relation to a larger norm of equality. A significant facet of modern multicultural settings has been the vociferous assertion of identity politics of various kinds (such as caste, race, gender, religion, sexuality, and so on), with each articulating a difference as well as lobbying for recognition of such differences, especially with regard to state policies. Perspectives that, until recently, downplayed differences in favor of cultural assimilation into a larger mainstream seem to have made way for a multicultural stance celebrating cultural difference today. It has been pointed out, however, that while it is true that to speak of the equality principle in a multicultural context is to actually recognize differences between groups, this always has to be contextually determined, for not all recognitions of difference yield themselves to an egalitarian principle (Hegde 2002). A contextualized view of equality is perhaps what is required today, evident, for example, in the numerous instances of positive discrimination with reference to caste groups, as well as in the reservations on the basis of identity markers such as religion or ethnic group, where equal representations are sought based on recognition of cultural difference and/or historical disprivilege. Though this strategy holds for representation of group rights in general, how do we tackle the question of internal differences within groups?

Amid avowedly multicultural contexts marked by the articulation of differences between groups, it appears that a number of intragroup differences and inequalities, such as those based on gender and sexual discrimination, could get obscured (Okin 1999). This danger has been recognized, for instance, in the debate on gender justice, particularly in the context of personal laws in India, where questions are raised as to whether a law bound to a religious patriarchal tradition could ensure justice for women. Conversely, suggestions of a uniform civil code have raised other problems such as those of the imposition of the patriarchal norms of majority cultures, or the attempt to extend an abstract vocabulary of rights without any consideration of the defining circumstances. Though configured differently, the problems posed by internal lines of differentiation within a group also arise when demands for the political representation for women are routed through caste or religious groups, creating confusion as to whom an elected woman is actually representing.

Two issues could be iterated at this juncture. One, in any society made up of a multiplicity of groups (as in India, or again increasingly in liberal democracies today), none of these groups is a monolith. Even within caste and religious groups there are several lines of differentiation such as on the basis of gender, status, and/or economic and political power, all of which would determine its relation to other groups. These principles of internal differentiation usually have a close link to cultural practices and ideologies obtaining in that community. Two, it is imperative, then, that we understand the symbiotic relations between gender and culture—the matrix of sexualization that was cited earlier on, for instance—for this could tell us something of the ways in which social life itself is sexualized within communities. Only a thorough and nuanced understanding of

such orderings would perhaps enable us to trace gender's interface with the equality principle and the transformations that each
undergoes subsequently.

REFERENCES

Agnes, F. (1992). Protecting women against violence? Review of a
decade of legislation, 1980–89. *Economic and Political Weekly*
27(11): WS19–30.

Balibar, E. (1994). Subjection and subjectivation. In *Supposing the Subject*, ed. J. Copjec, pp. 1–15. London: Verso.

Bock, G., and James, S., eds. (1992). *Beyond Equality and Difference: Citizenship, Feminist Politics and Female Subjectivity*. London: Routledge.

Chakravarty, U. (1989). Whatever happened to the Vedic Dasi?
Orientalism, nationalism and a script for the past. In *Recasting
Women: Essays in Colonial History*, ed. K. Sangari and S. Vaid,
pp. 27–87. New Delhi: Kali for Women.

Delhi University Forum for Democracy. (2001). *Women in Early India*.
Delhi.

Dumont, L. (1980). *Homo Hierarchicus: The Caste System and Its Implications*.
Chicago: University of Chicago Press.

Gandhi, N., and Shah, N. (1992). *The Issues at Stake: Theory and Practice in
the Contemporary Women's Movement in India*. New Delhi: Kali for
Women.

Gatens, M. (1992). Power, bodies and difference. In *Destabilizing Theory:
Contemporary Feminist Debates*, ed. M. Barrett and A. Phillips,
pp. 120–137. Stanford: Stanford University Press.

Hegde, S. (2002). Socio-cultural anthropology: conversational cross-
ings. Unpublished.

Hegde, S., and Niranjana, S. (1994). Of the religious and the (non-) feminine: open questions. *Contributions to Indian Sociology* 28(1): 107–122.

John, M. E., and Nair, J., eds. (1998). *A Question of Silence? The Sexual Economies of Modern India.* New Delhi: Kali for Women.

Kapur, R., and Cossman, B. (1996). *Subversive Sites: Feminist Engagements with Law in India.* New Delhi: Sage.

Kumar, R. (1993). *The History of Doing.* New Delhi: Kali for Women.

Marriott, M., ed. (1990). *India Through Hindu Categories.* New Delhi: Sage.

McNay, L. (2000). *Gender and Agency: Reconfiguring the Subject in Feminist and Social Theory.* Cambridge: Polity Press.

Menon, N., ed. (1999). *Gender and Politics in India.* New Delhi: Oxford University Press.

Mukhopadhyaya, M. (1998). *Legally Dispossessed: Gender, Identity and the Process of Law.* Calcutta: Stree.

Niranjana, S. (1994). On gender and difference: towards a re-articulation. *Social Scientist* 22(7–8):28–41.

———— (2001). *Gender and Space: Femininity, Sexualization and the Female Body.* New Delhi: Sage.

Okin, S. M. (1999). Is multiculturalism bad for women? In *Is Multiculturalism Bad for Women?*, ed. J. Cohen and M. Howard. Princeton, NJ: Princeton University Press.

Raheja, G. G., and Gold, A. G. (1996). *Listen to the Heron's Words: Reimagining Gender and Kinship in North India.* Delhi: Oxford University Press.

Ram, K. (1992). *Mukkuvar Women: Gender, Hegemony and Capitalist Transformation in a South Indian Fishing Community.* New Delhi: Kali for Women.

Ramanujan, A. K., ed. (1993). *Folktales from India.* New Delhi: Viking.

Rhode, D. L., ed. (1990). *Theoretical Perspectives on Sexual Difference.* New Haven, CT: Yale University Press.

Sangari, K. (1993). Consent, agency and rhetorics of incitement. *Economic and Political Weekly* 28(18):867–882.

Sangari, K., and Vaid, S., eds. (1989). *Recasting Women: Essays in Colonial History*. New Delhi: Kali for Women.

Scott, J. (1988). *Gender and the Politics of History*. New York: Columbia University Press.

Sundar Rajan, R. (1993). *Real and Imagined Women: Gender, Culture and Postcolonialism*. London: Routledge.

Thapan, M., ed. (1997). *Embodiment: Essays on Gender and Identity*. Delhi: Oxford University Press.

Tharu, S., and Niranjana, T. (1999). Problems for a contemporary theory of gender. In *Gender and Politics in India*, ed. N. Menon, pp. 494–526. New Delhi: Oxford University Press.

Williams, R. (1976). *Keywords: A Vocabulary of Culture and Society*. New York: Oxford University Press.

ABOUT THE AUTHORS

RAJA BEN SLAMA is a professor at the Faculté des Lettres, Manouba-Tunis, Tunis, Tunisia. His most recent book, in Arabic, is titled *The Ishq (Love-Desire) and Writing* (Dar al-Jamal, Cologne, 2003).

DRUCILLA CORNELL is a professor of law, women's studies, and political science at Rutgers University. She has authored several books, including *Between Women and Generations: Legacies of Dignity* (Palgrave Macmillan, 2002) and *Transformations: Recollective Imagination and Sexual Difference* (Routledge, 1993).

GENEVIÈVE FRAISSE is a philosopher and director of research at Centre National de la Recherche Scientifique. Author of numerous works, her work focuses on the history of the exchange between the sexes from an epistemological and political point of view. She has recently published *The Two Governments: The Family and The City* (Folio-Gallimard, 2001) and *The Controversy* (PUF, 2001).

SEEMANTHINI NIRANJANA is currently an independent researcher based in Hyderabad, India. She is presently working on legal rights and the constitution of sexual subjects in India. She has recently published a book entitled *Gender and Space: Femininity, Sexualization and the Female Body* (Sage, 2001).

LINDA WALDMAN is a social anthropologist and a research fellow in the Institute of Development Studies, University of Sussex, Sussex, England. Her many publicatons examine racial classification, identity, ritual, and gender. Her most recent work, "Houses and the Ritual Construction of Gendered Homes," appeared in *Journal of the Royal Anthropological Association*, vol. 9 (no. 4): 657–680, December, 2003.

LI XIAO-JIAN is a professor at the Center of Gender Studies, Da Lian University, Da Lian, China.